HARRY ANDERSON, ARTIST
COPYRIGHT © 1945 BY THE REVIEW AND HERALD

...n might be saved. John 3:17

Good
News
for
You

by ARTHUR S. MAXWELL

Author of *Your Bible and You, Courage for the Crisis,*
Time Running Out, The Bible Story, etc.

REVIEW AND HERALD PUBLISHING ASSOCIATION
WASHINGTON, D.C.

All the N.E.B. quotations throughout this book are from: *The New
English Bible*, New Testament. © The Delegates of the Oxford University Press and the Syndics of the Cambridge University Press 1961.

Excerpts from the Moffatt translation throughout are identified and
are: From: *The Bible: A New Translation* by James Moffatt. Copyright
by James Moffatt 1954. Used by permission of Harper & Row, Publishers,
Incorporated.

CONTENTS

"I have
good news for you:
there is great joy coming
to the whole people"

(Luke 2:10, N.E.B.)

Foreword

THERE is altogether too much bad news today. News about wars, riots, vandalism, sex crimes, and every other kind of violence. Newspapers are full of it; so are magazines and books. Remove it from radio and TV newscasts and little would be left but the advertisements.

People yearn for good news and rarely get it. Hence this volume, *Good News for You*. It is a volume of good cheer, straight from the Source of happiness.

To be honest, there is nothing new about it. It is as old as the hills. What makes it new is the fact that it has been buried under a heap of trash for such a long time.

Actually, this is a rediscovery of long-lost treasure, like salvaging gold and silver from a sunken Spanish galleon, or finding Europe's art treasures in the salt mines of Saxony after World War II.

Here is something that is as precious, as beautiful,

and as vital as it was when it disappeared, and it has lost none of its value and potency in the interim.

And it is *good* news—news to cheer the heart, comfort the soul, and pacify the mind. News that will change a person's outlook on life and make it seem worth living. It is so good that it sets the soul alight with new hope and ambition as the future becomes roseate with glowing possibilities and glorious challenges.

I have written this book for Christians and non-Christians alike, for those who belong to a church and those who have lost all interest in religion, whose reaction to all religious questions is "I couldn't care less."

Purposely I have tried to use the simplest language, convinced that one basic reason why the glorious good news of the Christian message has lost much of its potency is that it has become almost totally obscured and bogged down in theological jargon. If there is no reference in these pages to existentialism or neo-orthodoxy or demythologizing, or the like, I make no apology to anyone.

When Jesus spoke, the common people heard Him gladly, and it is my hope that millions of the common people of the twentieth century—and some not so common—will be blessed and refreshed by this new presentation of an old but ever-beautiful theme.

Here indeed is good news for *you.*

1

Great New Hope

"LET ME GO! I've nothing to live for!" cried a would-be suicide as a patrolman hauled him back over the balustrade of the Golden Gate Bridge.

His wife had left him, his children were in trouble, and he was heavily in debt. Taking his own life seemed the easy way out.

Many people feel like that today. Burdens seem too great. Nothing is really satisfying. Rewards are not worth the struggle. Life has become a bore.

Wages are higher than ever; there is more money about than ever; there are more cars and trailers and boats than ever; but who is content?

Millions rush hither and yon seeking happiness but never finding it. They try movies, theaters, dance halls, race courses, all in vain. Their search is never successful, and in their hearts they know it never will be.

Almost everybody you meet nowadays confesses to being "all wrought up" and "a bundle of nerves." Rare is the person who is not using aspirin or some more potent painkiller or headache pill. Fantastic quantities of tranquilizers are consumed every day, mostly by those who have misused their bodies in one way or another trying to get a "lift" without a letdown.

A deep sickness has gripped humanity, a sickness of the soul and the mind. Among its symptoms are the increase of degenerative diseases, the growth of alcoholism and drug addiction, the breakdown of morality, the decay of the home, and the spread of lawlessness. It can be seen, too, in the hideousness of modern art, in the wild, savage music that turns thousands of youth into shrieking maniacs, in the hatred that erupts in racial violence.

Like the Black Death of the Middle Ages this disease has spread from nation to nation until all the world is involved. Discontent, vandalism, and disrespect for law have become universal. The riots in Tokyo, Seoul, Singapore, Djakarta, Madras, Los Angeles, are all linked together. All are symptoms of the same inner dissatisfaction with life, the same vain belief that happiness can be achieved by physical and material means.

Something has gone wrong, terribly wrong. And the pity is that it has happened just when man is reaching the

Jesus, the only hope and safe arbiter of international peace, is portrayed here knocking for admittance on the offices of the United Nations in New York.

peak of his scientific triumphs. These are the years of the conquest of space. Men have orbited the earth times without number; Mariner IV has photographed Mars; rendezvous in space has been achieved; plans are on foot for the first expedition to the moon. Man's most glowing dreams are coming true.

This generation has also seen the conquest of the atom and the release of almost limitless energy, not only for destructive purposes but also for the lighting of cities, the powering of industry, and the making of fresh water from the sea. Never was there so much power available to man, for good or for ill.

If science could produce peace of mind and make people happy, the closing decades of the twentieth century would see a veritable heaven on earth. But it isn't working out that way. Each new discovery begets new rivalries and fears. The worst crime wave in history has come since the dawn of the space age.

Nor has the extravagant social planning of our time had much better results. Many countries have adopted the philosophy of the "welfare state," making abundant provision for everybody from the cradle to the grave, but apparently without increase in over-all contentment. In Sweden, where all the basic needs of the people, from cradle to grave, are underwritten by the state, the crime rate has gone up 97 per cent in the past fifteen years.

In the United States the Great Society is the rage of the moment, with astronomical sums being poured out to assist the aged, the sick, the needy, the illiterate. Not since Robin Hood has there been such a zealous effort to soak the rich to feed the poor. If money could bring in the golden age of universal peace and happiness, surely the current prodigal expenditures must succeed in so doing. But money alone will not do it, and cannot.

Significantly, at the very time Congress was voting billions for Medicare, frenzied people were throwing Molotov cocktails around in Los Angeles, burning down a large section of the city.

The deep sickness will not be healed with money, nor will lasting contentment be brought about by social programs. Money will help, of course; so will the social programs; but material means and methods alone will never satisfy the deeper yearnings of the human heart.

Only God can do that; and until man finds God again he will know no peace, nor any satisfying joy in life.

Money will not give it to him.

Alcohol will not give it to him.

Tobacco will not give it to him.

Sedatives will not give it to him.

Movies and theaters will not give it to him.

He must return to God, his Creator and Redeemer. Somehow he must find this true Friend, who loves and cares for him, and longs to help him.

"My help cometh from the Lord," said King David millenniums ago (Psalm 121:2). How right he was!

That is the only place anyone can get help, real help, on the basic issues of life. Only God, who made the human mind, can help a man think correctly, decide wisely, and live rightly.

This is the way—the only way—to peace of mind, contentment of spirit, and purposeful, joyful living.

Here is hope for the hopeless, rest for the weary, courage for the despondent.

This is the good news the world needs today.

If you are troubled, unhappy, overburdened, it is good news for you too. Wonderful news. The best news you ever heard.

Read on and discover what it may mean in your life.

2

Wonderful News

THIS IS NOT the first time in history that good news has been in great demand. Two thousand years ago when Rome ruled the world most of the empire was in need of good news. Palestine in particular was full of well-nigh hopeless people. Not only were most of them desperately poor but they had to endure all the indignities of foreign occupation. They lived in constant dread of punishment by their overlords, all too well aware how cruel and heartless they could be.

From time to time some had risen in revolt, only to be ruthlessly crushed. Now for the most part the populace waited and suffered in silence, for in very truth darkness covered the earth and "gross darkness the people."

A glimpse of their fears and muted hopes is revealed in the words of Zacharias at the naming of his son John (the Baptist): " 'Praise to the God of Israel! . . . Age

13

after age he proclaimed by the lips of his holy prophets, that he would *deliver us from our enemies, out of the hands of all who hate us;* that he would deal mercifully with our fathers, calling to mind his solemn covenant. Such was the oath he swore to our father Abraham, to *rescue us from enemy hands,* and grant us, *free from fear,* to worship him with a holy worship, with uprightness of heart, in his presence, our whole life long. And you, my child, you shall be called Prophet of the Highest, for you will be the Lord's forerunner, to prepare his way and lead his people to salvation through knowledge of him, by the forgiveness of their sins; for in the tender compassion of our God the morning sun from heaven will rise upon us, to *shine on those who live in darkness, under the cloud of death,* and to guide our feet into the way of peace' " (Luke 1:68-79, N.E.B.).

Here we glimpse the deepest longings of the people of that day. They wanted to be free—free from the Romans, free from fear, free from tyranny, free from "the cloud of death." They wanted to live in peace and happiness. But there was no sign as yet that their long-cherished hopes would ever be realized.

Then, all of a sudden, everything changed.

News of a Deliverer arrived, and it spread like wildfire across the country.

The story is told in the second chapter of the Gospel of Luke:

"Now in this same district [of Bethlehem] there were shepherds out in the fields, keeping watch through the night over their flock, when suddenly there stood before them an angel of the Lord, and the splendour of the Lord shone round them. They were terror-struck, but the angel said, 'Do not be afraid; *I have good news for you: there is great joy coming to the whole people.* Today in the city of David a deliverer has been born to you—the Messiah, the Lord. And this is your sign: you will find a baby lying all wrapped up, in a manger' " (verses 8-13, N.E.B.).

Then "all at once there was with the angel a great company of the heavenly host, singing the praises of God: 'Glory to God in highest heaven, and on earth his peace for men on whom his favour rests' " (verses 13, 14, N.E.B.).

Thrilled beyond words, the shepherds hurried into town and found the Babe in a manger, just as the angel had said.

It all seemed very wonderful until they began to reflect on the angel's message. How could this Baby deliver Israel? How could His birth be good news for "the whole people"?

Had the angel announced that Rome had been invaded and the emperor slain, that would have been something truly exciting. Had he disclosed a new plot to overthrow the hated overlords, had he revealed that an army of deliverance was on its way from Egypt or Mesopotamia, what great good news that would have been! But this Baby—what possible help could He be in a time like this?

Come to think of it, a baby must have seemed a most impractical solution to Israel's seemingly insoluble problems. What the subjugated nation wanted was a strong, virile, fearless leader who would issue a thrilling call to arms and drive the Romans into the Mediterranean. Now it was told that a baby had been born, a baby too weak to raise its head, a baby so poor it had to be born in a stable, a baby so low it didn't have a proper father—and this baby was going to be the long-hoped-for Deliverer!

No wonder many refused to accept the shepherds' story. It was too unreasonable, too altogether impossible of belief. Yet it was true. Everything happened just as the angel predicted.

This Baby *did* grow up to be the great Deliverer. He was no weakling, for within Him was the strength of the Omnipotent. Though He lived in poverty He owned the universe. And His Father was God.

He accomplished what the people hoped for, albeit in His own way and in His own time. He defeated the Romans, not by force of arms but by the power of love. By His Godlike life and teachings He changed the course of history and turned the world upside down.

Exactly as Zacharias prophesied, He delivered the people from fear of their enemies by proving that God is greater than all earthly powers and that His kingdom shall ultimately prevail.

He delivered them from fear of hardship and hunger by demonstrating that God is able to provide for every human need.

He delivered them from fear of sickness and disease by showing that God, the Source of all life, is both able and willing to heal.

He delivered them from fear of death by revealing His power to raise the dead.

He banished their hopelessness by revealing the glorious future God has planned for all who love Him.

Such was the "good news" the angel brought to the shepherds. Yet it was not for them only, or even for all Israel. It was for "the whole people." For everybody everywhere.

That Baby was not only the Messiah but also the Lord. He was indeed God, the Creator, who voluntarily, of His own free will and desire, became at that moment one with the human race.

2

Joseph and Mary, watching over the infant Saviour, hold Him forth for the adoration of the world's children.

Note the words in verse 13—"all wrapped up." What a significant and moving phrase! God Himself was "all wrapped up" in that manger. All the love of God, all the wisdom of God, all the power of God.

Here was a time bomb of enormous potency, with explosive force sufficient to blast the powers of evil into oblivion and to bring the whole ugly edifice of sin crashing down in ruin.

Here, too, was an infinitely powerful magnet, the most effective ever devised, magnetized with all the potency of divine compassion, strong enough to draw men back to God, back to holiness and righteousness and oneness with Him—and it was "all wrapped up" in that Baby.

Here also was a light of such brilliance that the like of it was never seen before on land or sea—a light able to illuminate the past, the present, and the future, and to direct all men in every part of this sin-cursed earth out of night into eternal day—and it was "all wrapped up" in that Baby.

Here also was the most powerful X-ray device ever conceived—capable of penetrating the innermost thoughts and motives of the human heart—and it was "all wrapped up" in that Baby.

Here, too, was an inexhaustible reservoir of hope and courage, "all wrapped up" in that Baby.

Here was a fountain of strength, sufficient for every human need, able to make the weakest of men "more than conquerors" over every temptation, and this, too, was "all wrapped up" in that Baby.

Here was limitless understanding and compassion, eager to forgive the worst of sinners and to accept the basest of men and women as sons and daughters of God and share with them, without question or discrimination, all the riches of the universe. This, too, was "all wrapped up" in that Baby.

What a precious package it was that Heaven laid on earth's doorstep on that far-off night in Bethlehem! How priceless was the treasure clothed in that frail and tiny form! How rich beyond imagination was the Gift placed in that manger!

But the good news became better as the marvelous package unfolded. Out of those swaddling clothes, out of that exquisite, divine chrysalis, came God Himself, to walk among men and show them how to live; to set them an example of happy, peaceful, untroubled, victorious living; to help them see how beautiful are God's thoughts, God's words, God's ways—so that men, women, and children would want to love Him and serve Him and please Him. Jesus came to assure everybody that God is not a harsh overlord but a kind, tenderhearted, forgiving, longsuffering Father, "not willing that any should perish."

He comforted the sorrowing, healed the sick, opened the eyes of the blind, gave hearing to the deaf and new hope to the worried and despairing.

Like a chime of silver bells, words of unexampled beauty flowed from His lips. "Peace I leave with you," He said, "my peace I give unto you: not as the world giveth, give I unto you. Let not your heart be troubled, neither let it be afraid" (John 14:27).

"Fear not, little flock; for it is your Father's good pleasure to give you the kingdom" (Luke 12:32).

"Come, ye blessed of my Father, inherit the kingdom prepared for you from the foundation of the world" (Matthew 25:34).

In all these and a hundred other lovely phrases God was thinking out loud, revealing Himself and His infinite concern for every member of the human race, joyfully telling of His glorious plans and purposes for them. He was drawing back the veil of the future, as only God can, to reveal the certain victory of right over wrong and the final triumph of all who love and serve Him.

Always He was the bearer of good news. To the blind He said, "See!" To the deaf, "Hear!" To the leper, "Be clean!" To the woman taken in adultery, "Neither do I condemn thee: go, and sin no more."

Even when evil men crucified Him, He still contrived to bring good news to those who watched and sorrowed.

His outstretched arms, nailed to the wooden beam, renewed His constant plea, now hereby emphasized a thousandfold, "Come unto me, all ye that labour and are heavy laden, and I will give you rest" (Matthew 11:28).

One of His nail-pierced hands pointed east, the other west, and together they cried, "As far as the east is from the west, so far hath he removed our transgressions from us" (Psalm 103:12).

Torn and bleeding though He was, He whispered words of pardon that have echoed down the centuries, from country to country, from continent to continent, all around the globe, "Father, forgive them; for they know not what they do" (Luke 23:34).

What a wealth of good news was in that angelic announcement to the shepherds! But look at it once more. Note its personal aspect. "I have good news for *you*." It was for each one of them. For everybody in Jerusalem. Everybody in Palestine. Everybody in the whole wide world. Everybody who should ever live. Everybody in every period of history, among every race, people, and nation from that day to the end of time.

This is where *you* come in. This good news is for *you*.

God came to this earth for *you*. He lived here for *you*. He died on the cross for *you*. He thinks of *you* and cares for *you* today, and will do so as long as you live. The peace and joy He offers everybody He offers *you*. The eternal life He offers everybody He offers *you*. The glorious home He is preparing is not only for all the saints but for *you*.

This is one of the greatest marvels of the gospel of Jesus Christ. It is so very personal. It assures us that while God loves everybody, He has profound, intimate, personal concern for every individual—every man, every woman, every boy, every girl. He loves each one for himself, for herself. It is within His capacity simultaneously to think of each one singly and alone, as if each one were the only being in the universe needing His help.

He thinks of us individually and cares for us individually and watches over us individually and plans for us individually. He has been doing this all our lives. He is doing it now. And He will do it tomorrow and always, if we will let Him.

Here is good news indeed.

3

God Isn't Dead

AT THIS point you may be saying, What about the statements made by certain scientists and clergymen that we've all been mistaken about God; that space exploration has proved that no such Being exists?

It is true that some well-known people have said just that. One of the Russian cosmonauts remarked that while orbiting the earth he looked for God and couldn't find Him. John A. T. Robinson, a Church of England bishop, declared in his book *Honest to God* that there's no place left for God anywhere. He is neither "up there" nor "out there." "In fact," he said, "the number of people who instinctively seem to feel that it is no longer possible to believe in God in the space-age shows how crudely physical much of this thinking about a God 'out there' has been. Until the last recesses of the cosmos had been explored or were capable of being explored (by radiotelescope if not by rocketry), it was still possible to locate God mentally in some *terra incognita.* But now it seems there is no room for him, not merely in the inn, but in the entire universe: for there are no vacant spaces left."— Pages 13, 14.

In Bishop Robinson's opinion the time has come for Christians to "grow up" and discard the concept of a personal God even though, he admits, this may mean throwing away most of the Bible and many long-cherished Christian beliefs.

As a matter of fact, there is little to distinguish his views from those of Julian Huxley, an acknowledged atheist, who is quoted by Dr. Robinson as saying, " 'It will soon be as impossible for an intelligent, educated man or woman to believe in a god as it is now to believe that the earth is flat.' "—*Ibid.,* p. 38.

But the fact that a Russian cosmonaut failed to find God in space, that preachers like Bishop Robinson no longer believe in a God "out there," and that outright atheists such as Huxley have completely dismissed Him from their thoughts, does not prove that God does not exist. He is not thus easily driven from His universe. All that these arguments mean is that these good men have absorbed what the apostle Paul aptly called "the wisdom of this world," which he equated with "folly."

"God has made the wisdom of this world look foolish," he wrote to the Corinthians. "As God in his wisdom ordained, the world failed to find him by its wisdom, and he chose to save those who have faith by the folly of the Gospel. Jews call for miracles, Greeks look for wisdom; but we proclaim Christ—yes, Christ nailed to the cross; and though this is a stumbling-block to Jews and folly to Greeks, yet to those who have heard his call, Jews and Greeks alike, he is the power of God and the wisdom of God" (1 Corinthians 1:21-24, N.E.B.).

The apostle's statement "the world failed to find him by its wisdom" is as true today as it was in the first century of the Christian Era. Now having failed to find Him, it is convinced that He does not exist.

As a matter of fact, however, there is more evidence today for the existence of a personal, omnipotent, omniscient God than ever before. Far from eliminating God from the universe, space-age discoveries have revealed more clearly than ever how vast is His wisdom, how limitless His power.

Astronomers, with their amazing new telescopes, have learned more in the past ten years about galaxies, suns, moons, planets, and other celestial bodies than had been known since the dawn of time. They have pressed back the frontiers of the universe by millions of light years only to be overwhelmed by the vastness, the orderliness, the majesty of it all. They may not have seen God, but they have seen indisputable evidence of the activity of a Master Architect, whose creation calls not only for wonderment but for reverence.

Highly skilled technicians and engineers, plotting the course of Mariner IV, the rendezvous of two spaceships, the trajectory of a moon rocket, or the thrust of a Titan booster, have found themselves face to face with absolute laws of nature they must perforce obey or fail in their enterprises. They have based all their calculations and the success of their billion-dollar undertakings upon the constancy of these laws and the split-second timing of moving bodies millions of miles apart. These topflight scientists may not have seen God, but they have certainly found themselves in the presence of an incredibly intelligent Lawmaker who not only conceived these highly complex rules and formulas but preserves them unchanged from age to age.

Biologists, with their electronic microscopes, have likewise learned more in the past decade about life in its many forms than was ever known before. They have probed mysteries that baffled their predecessors centuries ago. They have taken everything apart and examined it with elaborate care, even that greatest wonder of all, the single cell. They have found themselves on the verge of the secret of life itself and reached out, vainly, to grasp it. They may not have seen God, but they have found themselves face to face with marvels beyond their understanding—unmistakable evidence of skill, design, and wisdom that only an infinite Being could possess.

Zoologists have also had better opportunity to study animal life in the past few decades than was ever possible before. With modern methods and painstaking care they have followed the migration of birds and fish, and found themselves up against astonishing facts inexplicable apart from God. Some birds, such as the arctic tern, fly 22,000 miles a year. Others, like the white-throated warbler, that fly by night, set their course by the stars through some amazing device in their tiny heads.

By tagging eels it has been found that they make their way in adult life to the waters south of Bermuda where they lay their eggs and die; but their young move in two directions. Those hatched from eggs of the American species move west, while the offspring of the European species move east—but all, despite the difference in distances they have to travel, arrive at the river mouths when approximately three inches long!

Eagles' wings have been taken apart and examined microscopically to discover their secret of sustained flight.

Peacocks have been dissected to learn how they come to have such glorious feathers and how their amazing tail-erection system operates. Ostriches have been studied to find the secret of their fantastically beautiful plumes.

Those engaged in such research may not have seen God, but beyond all question they have witnessed the operation of a creative Mind that in some inexplicable way has imparted highly intelligent and skillful instincts to His creatures.

Physicians and surgeons, with fluoroscopes and other X-ray apparatus, have also learned more about the functioning of the human body in the past ten years than anyone knew before. Specialists of the highest caliber have concentrated upon the brain, the heart, the lungs, the digestive system, the nervous system, the reproductive organs. Yet even all this research has not fathomed all the mysteries of the marvelous mechanism of the human body. These men may not have seen God, but they have been confronted by overwhelming evidence that man is the masterpiece of an infinitely ingenious Creator.

Why cannot those who come so close to the works of God, who indeed almost tread in His footsteps, fail to see Him? Because, as the apostle Paul says, He is invisible—"the King of all worlds, immortal, invisible, the only God" (1 Timothy 1:17, N.E.B.).

Where is He then? "Up there?" "Out there?" Who knows? He has told us that He has a "dwelling place" but He hasn't told us where it is. It would seem reasonable to assume that He dwells at the center and heart of His universe, but if the universe is illimitable, where might that be?

We must be careful not to limit God—to say that the great and wonderful Creator must be here or there. I like David's glorious concept: "The heaven, even the heavens, are the Lord's: but the earth hath he given to the children of men" (Psalm 115:16).

As a young man I used to be bothered by questions about the nature and personality of God and the age-old question, What is God like? I would ask my friends, "When you pray, how do you think of God?" But no one gave me a satisfactory answer.

I used to think of those words of the Lord to Moses: "Thou canst not see my face: for there shall no man see me, and live" (Exodus 33:20), and wondered what the face of God was like. I thought, too, of that oft-repeated statement: "No man hath seen God at any time" (1 John 4:12), and wondered yet the more concerning Him.

I read also the apostle Paul's beautiful ascription of praise to "the blessed and only Potentate, the King of kings, and Lord of lords; who only hath immortality, dwelling in the light which no man can approach unto; whom no man hath seen, nor can see: to whom be honour and power everlasting" (1 Timothy 6:15, 16). What was one to make of that? How could one visualize an invisible God? Was I supposed to think of Him only as a blaze of light?

Then one day I read again these words of the apostle John: "No one has ever seen God; but God's only Son, he who is nearest to the Father's heart, he has made him known" (John 1:18, N.E.B.).

Suddenly a great light dawned. Here was the answer.

There is no need to struggle and strain to project one's mind into the insoluble mysteries of the infinite God. Christ has made Him known! "God was in Christ, reconciling the world unto himself" (2 Corinthians 5: 19). To know Christ is to know God.

This same problem once perplexed Philip. He felt that if only he could see the Father, he would be satisfied. " 'Show us the Father,' " he begged, " 'and we ask no more.' "

The Lord replied, " 'Have I been all this time with you, Philip, and you still do not know me? Anyone who has seen me has seen the Father. Then how can you say "Show us the Father"? Do you not believe that I am in the Father, and the Father in me? I am not myself the source of the words I speak to you: it is the Father who dwells in me doing his own work. Believe me when I say that I am in the Father, and the Father in me'" (John 14:8-11, N.E.B.).

Christ identified Himself completely with God. " 'My Father and I are one,' " He declared on another occasion (John 10:30, N.E.B.). Again He said: " 'When a man believes in me, he believes in him who sent me rather than in me; seeing me, he sees him who sent me'" (John 12:44, 45, N.E.B.).

Comforting words! The Invisible has revealed Himself; the Infinite has made Himself plain. No longer in confusion and perplexity do we need to wonder and question and doubt concerning Him. With full certainty of knowledge we may turn to Christ. We may touch as it were the wound prints in His hands and side, exclaiming with Thomas, "My Lord and my God!"

True, no photograph of Christ exists. As far as we know, no picture was ever painted of Him during His earthly sojourn. If there were, it no longer exists. Nevertheless, so complete and detailed is the story of His life that no Christian doubts that should he see his Saviour face to face he would recognize Him instantly.

By His brief life on earth Christ left an impression that will never be effaced from the memory of man. His

3

ministry of love and sacrifice stamped His portrait upon history. He left on record a revelation of God that all in every age might know and understand Him.

In revealing God, Christ brought to view all the qualities of the Father. He made Him known as the personification of righteousness, power, and love.

When in the long ago Jehovah descended in a cloud and passed before Moses, He proclaimed: "The Lord, The Lord God, merciful and gracious, longsuffering, and abundant in goodness and truth, keeping mercy for thousands, forgiving iniquity and transgression and sin, and that will by no means clear the guilty" (Exodus 34:6, 7).

That same loving Father was revealed by Christ. As the people listened to Him they were astonished; they had never understood that God was like this! They rejoiced when He said: "The Son of man is not come to destroy men's lives, but to save them" (Luke 9:56). They loved Him when He said: "The Son of man is come to seek and to save that which was lost" (Luke 19:10). And they marveled at His words, " 'God loved the world so much that he gave his only Son, that everyone who has faith in him may not die but have eternal life. It was not to judge the world that God sent his Son into the world, but that through him the world might be saved' " (John 3:16, 17, N.E.B.).

The apostle John, having listened to Jesus for three and a half years, came to the conclusion that "God is love" (1 John 4:8). Throughout those years he had heard God's voice. He had seen God in action. The eyes of the blind had been opened, the ears of the deaf unstopped. The sick had been healed, the lepers cleansed, even the dead raised to life. Miracle had succeeded miracle as Love poured itself out in sacrificial ministry to the poor and needy. "Never man spake like this man," the people said; and "He hath done all things well" (John 7:46; Mark 7:37).

God was in Christ making Himself known—wooing, loving, "reconciling the world unto himself," not willing that any should perish.

As men watched Christ, they beheld such goodness, such perfection, they were sure He must be God. This revelation of supreme love, perfect righteousness, flawless justice, illimitable power—surely this was divine.

So they worshiped Him. Christ accepted their worship. This was further evidence of His oneness with God.

Then came His death and resurrection. His ministry of reconciliation was crowned by Calvary. In that dreadful drama the revelation of God was perfected.

Love! Here was God in Christ dying for the ungodly; accepting unmerited death that others might live.

Righteousness! Here was God in Christ uplifting His holy law by His own obedience to death, and demonstrating to the entire universe its eternal inviolability.

Justice! Here was God in Christ accepting in Himself the penalty of man's transgression of His law—the Lawgiver dying for the lawless, the Judge for the criminal, the Just for the unjust.

Power! Here was God in Christ breaking the bands of death, storming the gates of hell, opening anew to the human family the way to the tree of life.

No wonder that "when the centurion, and they that were with him, watching Jesus, saw the earthquake, and those things that were done, they feared greatly, saying, Truly this was the Son of God" (Matthew 27:54).

No wonder, too, that the apostle Paul, writing shortly afterward, said of Christ: "Being in the form of God, [He] thought it not robbery to be equal with God: but made himself of no reputation, and took upon him the form of a servant, and was made in the likeness of men: and being found in fashion as a man, he humbled himself, and became obedient unto death, even the death of the cross. Wherefore God also hath highly exalted him, and given him a name which is above every name: that at the name of Jesus every knee should bow, of things in heaven, and things in earth, and things under the earth;

The centurion, witnessing the crucifixion of Jesus at Calvary, cried, "Truly this was the Son of God."

and that every tongue should confess that Jesus Christ is Lord, to the glory of God the Father" (Philippians 2: 6-11).

Death could not hold Him. From His sealed tomb He came forth its mighty conqueror. Reappearing to His disciples in bodily form, with "flesh and bones" (Luke 24:39), and bearing in His form the marks of His crucifixion (John 20:27), He at last ascended to heaven where, we are told, He "sat down on the right hand of the Majesty on high" (Hebrews 1:3).

There He remains, "the same yesterday, and to day, and for ever," awaiting the day of His promised glorious return, and "from henceforth expecting till his enemies be made his footstool" (Hebrews 13:8; 10:13).

Though we may not be able to understand all the mysteries of the Godhead, or penetrate the light with which God enshrouds Himself, yet we may know that at His right hand, seated upon His throne, coexistent with Him, is One with human form marked for eternity with the signs of His earthly sufferings.

Thither may our thoughts turn, not to some ethereal nothingness, not to "the ground of our being," but to a glorious high throne in the heavenly sanctuary, and to Him who sits thereon—to Christ, our Lord and our God.

What good news is this!

4

Bookful of Happiness

THERE IS more good news in the Bible than in any other book ever printed. It is radiant with hope and courage, a veritable bookful of happiness.

I am aware, of course, that there are those who say it is nothing but a collection of myths and legends. How mistaken they are! How much they lose!

When I was a very young man someone gave me H. L. Hastings' *Will the Old Book Stand?* and when I had finished reading it I was sure that the Bible would stand forever.

Wrote this famous evangelist—the Billy Graham of his day: "The Bible is a book which has been refuted, demolished, overthrown, and exploded more times than any other book you ever heard of. Every little while somebody starts up and upsets this book; and it is like upsetting a solid cube of granite. It is just as big one way as the other; and when you have upset it, it is right side up, and when you overturn it again, it is right side up still. Every little while somebody blows up the Bible; but when it comes down, it always lights on its feet, and runs faster than ever through the world.

"They overthrew the Bible a century ago, in Voltaire's time—entirely demolished the whole thing. In less than a hundred years, said Voltaire, Christianity will have been swept from existence, and will have passed into history. Infidelity ran riot through France, red-handed and impious. The century has passed away. Voltaire has 'passed into history,' and not very respectable history either; . . . but the word of God 'liveth and abideth forever.'"—*Will the Old Book Stand?* p. 11.

The same could be said of attacks upon the Bible today. They create a stir for a while, then pass away. Critics get big headlines but are soon forgotten. The Book lives on.

After all, there must be something very special about a volume that has lasted nineteen centuries, much of it longer than that.

There must be something very special about a book that has been translated into more than a thousand languages and is being translated into more and more languages all the time.

There must be something very special about a book that has been circulated by hundreds of millions of copies and still ranks among the world's best sellers.

There must be something very special about a book that fascinates theologians so much that they gather every few years to bring it up to date in a new version, such as the Revised Version, the Revised Standard Version, the Berkeley Version, the *New English Bible*, and many others—more than two hundred renderings of the New Testament alone since the days of Wycliffe.

There must be something very special about a book which has such a profound effect upon those who read it that it causes them to change their way of living, to give up bad habits and lead clean, noble, Christian lives.

There is. It is a divinely inspired Book, a "God-breathed" Book. Through its many authors God has spoken to the human race, revealing His plans and purposes for the world, His ideals and hopes for those who dwell in it. No one who reads it prayerfully can fail to hear His voice or feel the presence of His Holy Spirit.

I have been writing about the Bible for more than half a century and am more convinced than ever that it is the most wonderful Book ever written. Most impressive, I think, is the way it glows when a person studies it, as though there were some hidden fire within it that never goes out. Even the most familiar passage shines with new brilliance as one reads it for the tenth, the fiftieth, or maybe the hundredth time. Again and again one is compelled to say, "I never saw anything so beautiful before!"

In 1952 I began to "translate" the Bible for children, to put it into such simple language that the youngest child could see what a delightfully fascinating book it really is. The task took seven years, but proved to be the most rewarding of any I have ever undertaken. The Bible literally came to life for me, and, as time has proved, for many others. Hundreds of people have since written to tell me, "I never saw so much in the Bible before."

No wonder! I had never seen so much in it before myself! For those seven years the Book fairly shone with the glory of the Lord. And if the ten volumes of *The Bible Story* are blessing millions around the world today (they are now available in English, Spanish, French, and German) it is because of this inner power, this divine glow, which is the outstanding and most significant feature of the Word of God.

Time and again while writing these books I would be stalled for hours over a difficult passage. I would read it again and again, first in one version, then in another, seeking some way to simplify it, to bring its profound lesson out into the open where the youngest and most unlearned could see it clearly and revel in it. Without fail, sooner or later, the passage would begin to glow—sometimes so brilliantly that I would rush to my wife and say, "Did you ever see this in the Bible?" And she would say, with characteristic caution, "Are you sure it is really there?"

I recall struggling with the account of the raising of the widow's son, wondering how to make the story of a funeral attractive to youth. This is how it appears in the King James Version: "And it came to pass the day after, that he went into a city called Nain; and many of his disciples went with him, and *much people*. Now when he came nigh to the gate of the city, behold, there was a dead man carried out, the only son of his mother, and she was a widow: and *much people* of the city was with her. And when the Lord saw her, he had compassion on her, and said unto her, Weep not. And he came and touched the bier: and they that bare him stood still. And he said, Young man, I say unto thee, Arise. And he that was dead sat up, and began to speak. And he delivered him to his mother" (Luke 7:11-15).

Here was the story of a funeral procession and a kind deed to a poor widow. But was this all? No indeed.

Suddenly my attention was caught by the twice-repeated reference to "much people." "Much people" with Christ and "much people" with the widow.

Glorious thought! Here were *two* processions. One made up of Jesus and His disciples, the other of the poor widow and the mourners. One was moving into the city of Nain, the other out of it. One was led by the Prince of life, the other by a corpse. One was a procession of joy, the other of sorrow. All at once they met—and life triumphed over death.

Truly it was a funeral procession, but not a funeral. The funeral was interrupted as life from the Son of God swept through the lifeless form of the young man. And this is what Jesus came to do for all mankind—to make funerals forever obsolete by banishing death for all eternity.

Another passage that "glowed" in a special way for me was Luke 23:50-53. In the King James Version it reads like this: "And, behold, there was a man named Joseph, a counsellor; and he was a good man, and a just: (The same had not consented to the counsel and deed of them;) he was of Arimathaea, a city of the Jews: who also himself waited for the kingdom of God. This man went unto Pilate, and begged the body of Jesus. And he took it down, and wrapped it in linen, and laid it in a sepulchre that was hewn in stone, wherein never man before was laid."

At first this appears to be merely a brief report of what happened to the body of Jesus immediately after the crucifixion; but then I compared it with John 19: 38-40. All of a sudden one passage set the other alight, until both shone with heavenly radiance.

I saw a ladder placed against the cross. An old man is climbing it, while another waits anxiously below. Now the man on the ladder draws out the nails. But he needs help. The body is falling. So another ladder is raised. The second man climbs it. Together, very gently, they lower the Master to the ground, His limp arms around their necks as though He were saying to them, "Thank you, friends, for coming; thank you for helping Me."

What a beautiful thought! When His own special friends had forsaken Him and fled, these two old men, these "secret disciples," came to His aid! Even more thrilling is the realization that though someone who hated Jesus drove in the nails, someone who loved Him pulled them out!

Another radiant glow appeared as I was poring over John 21:9-13, which reads as follows: "As soon then as they were come to land, they saw a fire of coals there, and fish laid thereon, and bread. Jesus saith unto them, Bring of the fish which ye have now caught. Simon Peter went up, and drew the net to land full of great fishes, an hundred and fifty and three: and for all there were so many, yet was not the net broken. Jesus saith unto them, Come and dine. And none of the disciples durst ask him, Who art thou? knowing that it was the Lord. Jesus then cometh, and taketh bread, and giveth them, and fish likewise."

Was this merely the record of Jesus' last meeting with His disciples in Galilee? Or could it have a deeper meaning?

That is when I noticed the fire on the beach. Who lighted it? Jesus, of course. Who else? Not for Himself, but for His cold, weary disciples who had fished all night and caught nothing.

And He had "fish laid thereon." Who had caught them? He had, of course. Who else? How kind and thoughtful of Him to provide this food at such an early hour!

But the best was yet to come. For Jesus didn't say "Come and dine" but "Come and have breakfast," as most modern versions render the phrase.

How delightful! Jesus, the Lord of life, just risen from the dead, asked His earthly friends to have breakfast with Him. And as breakfast is the first meal of the day, even so that meal marked not only the beginning of a new day for the disciples but a whole new life for them. Fishing on Galilee for them was over forever. From then on they would go forth to "catch" men for the kingdom of God.

When in course of time I came to Acts 9:36-42 this passage also glowed with a glory I shall never forget. It concerns Dorcas and reads like this:

"Now there was at Joppa a certain disciple named Tabitha, which by interpretation is called Dorcas: this woman was full of good works and almsdeeds which she did. And it came to pass in those days, that she was sick, and died: whom when they had washed, they laid her in an upper chamber. And forasmuch as Lydda was nigh to Joppa, and the disciples had heard that Peter was there, they sent unto him two men, desiring him that he would not delay to come to them.

"Then Peter arose and went with them. When he was come, they brought him into the upper chamber: and all the widows stood by him weeping, and shewing the coats and garments which Dorcas made, while she was with them. But Peter put them all forth, and kneeled down, and prayed; and turning him to the body said, Tabitha, arise. And she opened her eyes: and when she saw Peter, she sat up. And he gave her his hand, and lifted her up, and when he had called the saints and widows, presented her alive."

What could I do with this? I wondered. How retell it in a way that would make it interesting to children? Was it not just the story of a dear old lady who made clothes for the poor and started the first Dorcas Society?

That's when I noticed that Dorcas was not this lady's real name, but her nickname. Peter called her Tabitha, but the local people, who loved her so much, called her Dorcas. Why Dorcas?

I looked in the margin and read that Dorcas meant "doe," which is another name for a deer, a gazelle, or an antelope.

Suddenly light dawned. And what a light!

Tabitha was not an old lady at the point of death. On the contrary, she was young, vigorous, enthusiastic, ever running from one needy person to another. "She's quick as a gazelle," the church members said. "She hurries about town like an antelope. Let's call her Dorcas." And the name stuck to her.

She didn't die of old age. I should say not! She worked herself to death caring for others. That's why Peter raised her from the dead. The little church needed her desperately. So did God.

Thus does the Bible glow. And it will glow for you, too, if you will take time to read it.

Frankly, I think this is the greatest proof of the Bible's

inspiration. Historical and prophetical evidences are important, and should be given their full weight, but the greatest test of any book's inspiration is its effect upon those who read it. An inspired book will inspire its readers. It will set their souls on fire for God.

And that is exactly what the Bible does. It stimulates the mind, uplifts the thoughts, and sets the heart aglow.

Regarded thus, it becomes in very truth a bookful of happiness—of good news about God, about the future, about the world we live in, about the problems that beset us in our daily living.

More and more people are finding it so, Protestants and Catholics alike, and people who don't belong to any denomination at all. The Bible speaks to all without discrimination. Its message of joy and courage—of faith, hope, and love—is for everybody of every race and color and nation around the world.

Toward the close of 1965 I attended the final session of Vatican II in Rome. Fortunately, my visit coincided with discussion of the Declaration on Divine Revelation, the document dealing with the place of the Bible in the church today. In the final draft of this document I read this striking affirmation of the inspiration of the Bible:

The church "holds that the books of both the Old and New Testament in their entirety, with all their parts,

4

are sacred and canonical because, having been written under the inspiration of the Holy Spirit . . . they have God as their author. . . . In composing the sacred books, God chose men and while employed by Him they made use of their powers and abilities, so that with Him acting in them and through them, they, as true authors, consigned to writing everything and only those things which He wanted.

"Therefore, since everything asserted by the inspired authors or sacred writers must be held to be asserted by the Holy Spirit, it follows that the books of Scripture must be acknowledged as teaching firmly, faithfully, and without error that truth which God wanted put into the sacred writings for the sake of our salvation."—WALTER M. ABBOTT, S.J., ed., *The Documents of Vatican II*, pp. 118, 119.

Concerning the books of the Old Testament this document says that they "reveal to all men the knowledge of God and of man and the ways in which God, just and merciful, deals with men. These books . . . give expression to a lively sense of God, contain a store of sublime teachings about God, sound wisdom about human life, and a wonderful treasury of prayers, and in them the mystery of our salvation is present in a hidden way. Christians should receive them with reverence."—*Ibid.*, p. 122.

The disciple of Christ, then, ought to read them carefully, "particularly since they give excellent expression to a vivid sense of the most holy and most merciful God."

Concerning the New Testament, this document says that "the four Gospels . . . whose historical character the Church unhesitatingly asserts, faithfully hand on what Jesus Christ, while living among men, really did and taught for their eternal salvation until the day He was taken up into heaven. . . . The sacred authors wrote the four Gospels, selecting some things from the many which had been handed on by word of mouth or in writing, . . . always in such fashion that they told us the honest truth about Jesus. . . ."

"Besides the four Gospels," it goes on to say, "the canon of the New Testament also contains the Epistles of St. Paul and other apostolic writings, composed under the inspiration of the Holy Spirit. In these writings, by the wise plan of God, those matters which concern Christ the Lord are confirmed, His true teaching is more and more fully stated, the saving power of the divine work of Christ is preached, the story is told of the beginnings of the Church and her marvelous growth, and her glorious fulfillment is foretold."—*Ibid.*, p. 124.

"Easy access to sacred Scripture should be provided for all the Christian faithful," the document continues.

"The word of God should be available at all times."
Therefore the church encourages the study of the Holy
Scriptures so that "as many ministers of the divine word as
possible will be able effectively to provide the nourish-
ment of the Scriptures for the people of God, thereby en-
lightening their minds, strengthening their wills, and
setting men's hearts on fire with the love of God."—*Ibid.*,
p. 126.

Toward the close of the document the council "earnestly and especially urges all the Christian faithful . . .
to learn by frequent reading of the divine Scriptures the
'excelling knowledge of Jesus Christ' (Philippians 3:
8). 'For ignorance of the Scriptures is ignorance of Christ.'
. . . And let them remember that prayer should accompany
the reading of sacred Scripture, so that God and man may
talk together."—*Ibid.*, p. 127.

Coming from Vatican II, these words will surely encourage all Catholics to study their Bibles with a new
spirit of inquiry and hope, while at the same time they will
remind Protestants of their claim since the Reformation
that "the Bible and the Bible only" is their rule of faith.

No matter to which Christian body you happen to belong, or whether you haven't as yet chosen any particular
church as your own, the rich treasures of the Bible are
yours to enjoy any time, anywhere.

5

No Need to Fear

MOST PEOPLE are full of fears today. If it's not one thing it's another.

Many are afraid that some minor war will escalate into a major global conflict, with all its human misery, higher taxes, and interruption of personal plans and pleasures.

Others are sure someone is about to set off a nuclear device and plunge the world into an international holocaust.

Fear of inflation and the resultant devaluation of money is also ever present today, as is fear of accident, sickness, and other catastrophes that can so swiftly bring financial disaster.

Fear of race riots and other civil disorders is increasingly prevalent, as well as fear of hoodlums and undisciplined youth.

If you are plagued with any or all of these fears, here is good news for you. You can be rid of them now. You can exchange them for peace of mind by one simple act of faith.

The Bible says, "Great peace have they which love thy law: and nothing shall offend them" (Psalm 119: 165). "They shall have no stumblingblock" is the marginal reading.

In other words, nothing will upset them.

If God is your Friend—if you love Him sincerely and find happiness in trying to please Him, you will be saved all the worries that beset those who never give God a thought.

Things that upset them won't bother you.

Problems that give them ulcers won't affect your health.

Why?

Because your decision to do God's will identifies you with Him. Your love for Him brings you as close to Him as a son to his father or a daughter to her mother. When trouble looms or danger threatens He moves in to help you. He is always "in the shadows," keeping watch over His own.

If you are a father or mother you will understand what I mean. Aren't you always alert to your children's needs, ready to help them in any emergency to the best of your ability? Of course you are. So is God.

David had the right idea when he wrote: "Leave all to him, rely on him, and he will see to it. . . . Leave it to the Eternal and be patient" (Psalm 37:5, 7, Moffatt).

"Roll thy way upon the Lord" is the marginal reading of this passage in the King James Version. The meaning is the same. Whatever your burden or fear, roll it upon God, confident that He loves you, cares for you, plans for you. The very thought that the omnipotent, all-wise God, Creator of all the wonders of nature, is concerned for your welfare will dispel the worst of fears.

There is an intimate connection between trust in God and peace of mind. They go together.

King David understood this basic principle of life better than any other old Testament character.

"Though I walk through the valley of the shadow of death," he wrote, "I will fear no evil: for thou art with me" (Psalm 23:4).

The sense of God's nearness gave him peace.

Again, in Psalm 27:1 he wrote: "The Lord is my light and my salvation; whom shall I fear? the Lord is the strength of my life; of whom shall I be afraid?"

Growing bolder still, he wrote in Psalm 46:1: "God is our refuge and strength, a very present help in trouble.

Therefore will not we fear, though the earth be removed, and though the mountains be carried into the midst of the sea."

Equally beautiful is this brief statement of his faith: "The Lord is on my side; I will not fear: what can man do unto me?" (Psalm 118:6).

Without doubt, he had many moments of worry during his long and eventful life—as when he fled from Saul, or when his son, Absalom, attempted to wrest the kingdom from him; but these do not minimize his great declarations of confidence in God. Through every trying experience he continued to trust in his lifelong Friend, and in every case peace returned to him.

So it may be with you. You can't avoid fears and worries. Of course not. Nobody can. But if you trust God and roll your burdens upon Him, they will never "get you down."

Isaiah understood this. From a wealth of experience he declared, "Thou wilt keep him in perfect peace, whose mind is stayed on thee: because he trusteth in thee. Trust ye in the Lord for ever: for in the Lord Jehovah is everlasting strength" (Isaiah 26:3, 4).

Dr. Moffatt renders it thus: "Thou dost protect and prosper steadfast souls, for they rely on thee. Always rely on the Eternal, for the Eternal's strength endures."

Either way, this text is a most beautiful expression of the great truth that God gives peace of mind to those who rely on Him.

Also through Isaiah, God gave this glorious assurance to His people: "Fear thou not; for I am with thee: be not dismayed; for I am thy God: I will strengthen thee; yea, I will help thee; yea, I will uphold thee with the right hand of my righteousness" (Isaiah 41:10).

What a lovely promise to claim in these turbulent times!

Here is another: "Fear not: for I have redeemed thee, I have called thee by thy name; thou art mine. When thou passest through the waters, I will be with thee; and through the rivers, they shall not overflow thee; when thou walkest through the fire, thou shalt not be burned; neither shall the flame kindle upon thee" (Isaiah 43:1, 2).

In my Bible this passage is underlined in red—and has been for more than fifty-five years. As a boy I was caught by an incoming tide and needed help desperately, and God came to the rescue, just in time. With the thoughtlessness of youth I attempted to cross a mile-wide ford between two islands of the Outer Hebrides without asking anyone about the tides. As I reached the middle, half a mile from either shore, I noticed that the tide had

PAINTING BY HARRY BAERG   © 1964 BY REVIEW AND HERALD →

The author of *Good News for You,* endeavoring to cross the ocean current to an island on the other side, was miraculously saved from death at high tide.

turned and the sea was rushing in. Breathing a prayer, I strode ahead as the waters rose higher and higher, clear to my neck. Another minute or so and I would have been swept away by the fierce current.

"Guide my feet!" I prayed. And God did. Gradually, as I struggled toward the farther shore, the water became shallower, and at last I emerged unharmed. But for a while it was touch and go; and for my deliverance on that far-off afternoon I shall be forever grateful.

That experience taught me something. It let me know *personally* that God's promises can be relied upon, that He cares for *me*.

It was a personal experience that first caused Isaiah to sense the guiding and keeping power of God and led him in later years to write so fervently about the blessings that await those who trust Him fully.

When he was a very young man he saw God in a vision that molded the rest of his life.

H. BAERG

"In the year that king Uzziah died," he wrote, "I saw also the Lord sitting upon a throne, high and lifted up, and his train filled the temple" (Isaiah 6:1).

That was about 740 B.C. Uzziah's fifty-two-year reign as king of Judah had just ended and everybody was worried about the future.

Fearing attack by the Assyrians, the Egyptians, and the Philistines, the late king had "strengthened himself exceedingly." He had "built towers in Jerusalem" and "towers in the desert." He had assembled also a well-organized army of some three hundred thousand men who "went out to war by bands" and "made war with mighty power." He had provided weapons in abundance, including "shields, and spears, and helmets, and habergeons, and bows, and slings to cast stones." He had also ordered the making of new methods of warfare, such as "engines, invented by cunning men," which were set up on the towers and bulwarks of the city "to shoot arrows and great stones withal." See 2 Chronicles 26:8-15.

All these armaments brought no one peace of mind. Always the question remained, Are they strong enough?

Then, as now, there never seemed to be quite enough protection, especially with Tiglath-pileser III on the Assyrian throne. That shrewd and powerful monarch seemed bent on conquering all Western Asia, and his military expeditions were coming ever closer to Judah.

Then Uzziah died. Judah's fear can be imagined. Would Tiglath-pileser seize this opportunity to move south and wipe out the little nation before it could recover from the passing of its strong and trusted leader? Jotham, heir to the throne, was only twenty-five. How could he stand up to the great conqueror who had already carried many thousands of Israelites into captivity?

It was at this time of grave perplexity and general alarm that Isaiah saw the Lord "sitting upon a throne, high and lifted up" while seraphim cried one to another, "Holy, holy, holy, is the Lord of hosts."

What a moment to see God! Judah's throne might be vacant, but God's was not. He was still Monarch of all, and ever would be. Unchanged and unchanging through unending years, He would reign serenely forever and ever, from everlasting to everlasting.

On earth there might be fear and uncertainty, but not in heaven. There, amid indescribable calm, angels sang of the glorious majesty of the Most High.

Earthly thrones might totter, kingdoms rise and fall, but the throne of God remained inviolate and undisturbed, to endure through all generations. And from this throne, unmoved by human turmoil and clamor, God would direct the affairs of nations with justice and judgment until His eternal purpose should be consummated.

If up to this moment Isaiah had been distressed over the course of events, his concern was now at an end. Fortified by this vision he was able to face the perils ahead with confidence. Trusting God completely, he accepted his divine commission with the words "Here am I; send me" (Isaiah 6:8).

In a time of grave perplexity Moses was given a similar vision (Exodus 24:10), as also was the prophet Micaiah (1 Kings 22:19), and Amos the dedicated herdsman (Amos 9:1). Years later, during the Babylonian captivity, both Daniel (Daniel 7:9) and Ezekiel (Ezekiel 1:1; 10:1-5) saw visions of the Lord upon His throne, as also did John on the Isle of Patmos during the persecution of the early church. See Revelation 4:1-6.

These records suggest that in times of special need, when trials and perils abound, a glimpse of God upon His throne is sufficient to banish fear and restore both hope and courage to the heart.

You and I may not witness the same dazzling scenes of glory that the prophets of old beheld, but just turning our thoughts heavenward can accomplish the same result.

"Lift up your eyes!" is a frequent Biblical exhortation, and it is excellent counsel today. We need to look up from the events and conditions that trouble us, and tell ourselves that God not only knows about them but is more concerned than we could possibly be. The very thought that He is in control, leading and directing according to His infinite wisdom, will give us equanimity of spirit and renew our courage.

In the midst of his long reign, Nebuchadnezzar was given seven years of punishment for his pride and vainglory. At its conclusion he declared: "At the end of the days I, Nebuchadnezzar, lifted my eyes to heaven, and my reason returned to me, and I blessed the Most High, and praised and honored him who lives for ever; for his dominion is an everlasting dominion, and his kingdom endures from generation to generation; all the inhabitants of the earth are accounted as nothing; and he does according to his will in the host of heaven and among the inhabitants of the earth; and none can stay his hand or say to him, 'What doest thou?'" (Daniel 4:34, 35, R.S.V.).

This heathen monarch did not see God as did the prophets of Israel, but lifting his eyes heavenward brought him healing and new hope. His reason returned to him. His judgment was no longer impaired. He saw everything in a new light. Humbly recognizing God's sovereignty over men and nations, he cried, "Now I,

Nebuchadnezzar, praise and extol and honor the King of heaven; for all his works are right and his ways are just; and those who walk in pride he is able to abase" (verse 37).

As a result he returned to his royal duties, renewed in body and soul, and still more greatness was added to him.

Daniel in the lions' den was granted no special vision of God, but evidence is plentiful that this good man took his eyes off the lions and turned them heavenward. In so doing he found the help he so desperately needed. Next morning when King Darius came to the den to inquire concerning his safety the prophet replied, "My God sent his angel and shut the lions' mouths, and they have not hurt me" (Daniel 6:22, R.S.V.).

Then it was that the king "wrote to all the peoples, nations, and languages that dwell in all the earth: 'Peace be multiplied to you. I make a decree, that in all my royal dominion men tremble and fear before the God of Daniel, for he is the living God, enduring for ever; his kingdom shall never be destroyed, and his dominion shall be to the end. He delivers and rescues, he works signs and wonders in heaven and on earth, he who has saved Daniel from the power of the lions'" (verses 25-28).

There is a mighty blessing in the upward look. Just thinking about God in a moment of crisis can mean all the difference between cringing fear and holy boldness, for He is the fountain of courage, the never-failing source of Christian fortitude.

No one knew this better than that stalwart Christian leader the apostle Paul. On his last visit to Jerusalem, though warned again and again of "bonds and afflictions" awaiting him, he refused to be intimidated. "None of these things move me," he said, "neither count I my life dear unto myself, so that I might finish my course with joy, and the ministry, which I have received of the Lord Jesus, to testify the gospel of the grace of God" (Acts 20:24).

The upward look sustained him. His worst trials he adjudged of little account as he let his mind dwell upon the Lord he loved, seated "on the right hand of the Majesty on high" (Hebrews 1:3). Utterly convinced that the King of the universe was his friend, he feared nothing and nobody.

He had troubles innumerable—enough to crush the spirit of the bravest. Think what he suffered:

"Of the Jews five times received I forty stripes save one," he told the church at Corinth. "Thrice was I beaten with rods, once was I stoned, thrice I suffered

5

shipwreck, a night and a day I have been in the deep; in journeyings often, in perils of waters, in perils of robbers, in perils by mine own countrymen, in perils by the heathen, in perils in the city, in perils in the wilderness, in perils in the sea, in perils among false brethren; in weariness and painfulness, in watchings often, in hunger and thirst, in fastings often, in cold and nakedness. Beside those things that are without, that which cometh upon me daily, the care of all the churches" (2 Corinthians 11:24-28).

Did all this bring him to despair? No indeed.

With amazing spiritual buoyancy he wrote: "We are troubled on every side, yet not distressed; we are perplexed, but not in despair; persecuted, but not forsaken; cast down, but not destroyed. . . . For which cause we faint not; but though our outward man perish, yet the inward man is renewed day by day. For our light affliction, which is but for a moment, worketh for us a far more exceeding and eternal weight of glory; while we look not at the things which are seen, but at the things which are not seen: for the things which are seen are temporal; but the things which are not seen are eternal" (2 Corinthians 4:8-18).

The New English Bible renders verses 16-18 thus: "No wonder we do not lose heart! Though our outward humanity is in decay, yet day by day we are inwardly renewed. Our troubles are slight and short-lived; and their outcome an eternal glory which outweighs them far. Meanwhile our eyes are fixed, not on the things that are seen, but on the things that are unseen: for what is seen passes away; what is unseen is eternal."

Here Paul revealed the secret of his indomitable spirit. By faith he looked beyond the troubles that surrounded him, and fastened his gaze upon the throne of God, finding there an inexhaustible reservoir of strength and courage. No wonder he did not lose heart!

Perhaps the most striking example of his fortitude under stress occurred during his last voyage across the Mediterranean as a prisoner of the Romans. Not far from Crete the ship, with 276 persons aboard, ran into a heavy storm. For several days and nights the tempest raged, battering the vessel so severely that both crew and passengers lost all hope of seeing land again.

Then, as the ship pitched and rolled amid the giant combers, this man of God somehow made his way to where most of the terrified crew and seasick passengers were gathered and brought them this heartening message:

"I urge you not to lose heart; not a single life will be lost, only the ship. For last night there stood by me an angel of the God whose I am and whom I worship. 'Do not be afraid, Paul,' he said; 'it is ordained that you shall appear before the Emperor; and, be assured, God has granted you the lives of all who are sailing with you.' So keep up your courage: I trust in God that it will turn out as I have been told" (Acts 27:22-25, N.E.B.).

And that is how it did turn out. His courage and God's providence carried the whole ship's company to safety on the island of Malta.

He saw no glowing vision of the throne of God as did Isaiah or Ezekiel in years long past, but he believed with all his heart that God was in complete control of the situation—just as you and I can believe today. "We walk by faith, not by sight," he said (2 Corinthians 5:7), or, as *The New English Bible* renders this passage: "Faith is our guide, we do not see him."

Such may be your experience too. God is as willing to help you as He was to help any of the great men of Bible times. He is the same "yesterday, and to day, and for ever" (Hebrews 13:8). His love is so limitless that it takes in everybody of every age, every country, every race, every tongue. It takes in you, with all your troubles and problems and fears.

Whatever happens, remember that He loves you and is concerned about you.

Today He says to you, as to His disciples in the long ago, " 'Are not sparrows five for twopence? And yet not one of them is overlooked by God. More than that, even the hairs of your head have all been counted. Have no fear; you are worth more than any number of sparrows' " (Luke 12:6, 7, N.E.B.).

" 'Therefore' "—and how appropriate are His words to our present needs—" 'I bid you put away anxious thoughts. . . . Think of the ravens: they neither sow nor reap; they have no storehouse or barn; yet God feeds them. You are worth far more than the birds! . . .

" 'Think of the lilies: they neither spin nor weave; yet I tell you, even Solomon in all his splendour was not attired like one of these. But if that is how God clothes the grass, . . . how much more will he clothe you! . . .

" 'You are not to worry. For all these are things for the heathen to run after; but you have a Father who knows that you need them. No, set your mind upon his kingdom, and all the rest will come to you as well.

" 'Have no fear, little flock; for your Father has chosen to give you the Kingdom' " (Luke 12:22-32, N.E.B.).

What good news is this!

Life without worry, life without fear, and the kingdom of God thrown in!

6

No Need to Despair

WHEN PRESIDENT KENNEDY was assassinated all the world mourned. Protestants and Catholics alike wept openly at the tragic passing of this friendly, high-minded young man who had captured everybody's heart.

When Sir Winston Churchill was laid to rest millions followed his funeral cortege on TV with tear-dimmed eyes, aware that with this very great man had passed an epoch, a way of life, that would never be seen again.

Such mourning is natural, but temporary. Within hours it merges into regret tinged with sadness.

Sorrow comes closer and lasts longer when it enters the family circle, as when death claims a revered father, a beloved mother, a son or a daughter in the prime of life, a much-loved child, or a lifelong friend.

Thousands of visitors pay tribute to the memory of former President J. F. Kennedy, whose body is buried in this inclosure at Arlington National Cemetery.

At such times the anguish can be almost unbearable, bordering on despair. The loss seems so cruel, so needless, so irreparable, so eternal. Those left behind feel completely frustrated, utterly helpless, amid the wreckage of their hopes and dreams.

Grief over such disasters may not be as publicly demonstrated as it used to be, but it is equally real and painful. In most places outward signs of mourning, such as veils and widow's weeds, black arm bands, and crepe-hung doorways have gone the way of the elaborate hearse pulled by plumed horses. People tend to mourn "covertly, by subterfuge," in various "degrees of depression," says one writer. If they despair they keep it to themselves.

In his book *Death, Grief and Mourning,* Dr. Geoffrey Gorer tells of his brother's widow whose emotional reticence led her to refuse to manifest any outward signs of mourning. As a result, "she let herself be, almost literally, eaten up with grief, sinking into a deep and long-lasting depression."

Striving to cover grief does not end it. Instead, this tends to drive it "underground," to do a deadly work within the mind.

"Many a widow," says Dr. Gorer, "invited to a party to 'take her mind off things' has embarrassed herself and her hostess by a flood of tears at the height of the festivities." All who have suffered a specially sad separation will understand this perfectly. No party, however gay, can assuage a great sorrow. Despair is hard to hide.

Part of the trouble nowadays may well lie in the changing public attitude to death. This results, says *Time* magazine,* from the multiplication of old people's homes and hospitals so that "dying is done offstage; gone are the hushed house, the doctor's visits, the solemn faces, the deathbed scenes that put death in life's perspective. Children of the TV generation are such strangers to natural death that on hearing that Grandfather is dead, they have been known to ask: 'Who shot him?' . . .

"Once the old liturgies asked God's protection from a sudden death; today it is expected that people hope to die suddenly. And they do. In automobiles and airplanes, through war or crime, death comes ever more abruptly, ever more violently. And after middle age, it comes suddenly through heart attack or stroke. There is hardly time to put one's life in order, in the ancient phrase, and to prepare for the end. In many a modern dying, there is no moment of death at all. Without realizing the momentous thing that is happening to them, patients are eased into the long, final coma."

Another aspect is the fact that "religiously, the prom-

---

* November 12, 1965, p. 52, essay "On Death as a Constant Companion."

ise of immortality has become dim and uncertain." Death is regarded as "a banal accident in an indifferent universe." Modern man "is especially troubled by the prospect of a meaningless death and a meaningless life—the bleak offering of existentialism." He sees death as a "trap door to nothingness."

Such concepts offer no balm to broken hearts. They staunch no tears. They bring no hope to the despairing. Nor do they provide answers to the eternal questions: What is death? Why did my loved one have to die? Where is he now? Shall I ever see him again?

No wonder people seek to hide their grief, preferring to suffer alone and out of sight. They don't know where to go for help. "Go to a party and forget" is often the only advice they get. And frankly, if death were indeed only a "trap door to nothingness," it might be the best thing to do.

Better counsel, however, is available. If you, perchance, are on the verge of despair, grieving over the loss of some dear one; if you are sad, fearful, confused, heartbroken, God has good news for you.

This too comes from the Bible, where so much good news is found. And it is as meaningful and comforting as when first recorded hundreds of years ago. Let me point it out.

First, about death—when and why it started and what it really is. As a matter of fact, death isn't as old as you may think it is. It is not even as old as the human race. It first began to plague man some time after his creation, and then only as a direct result of his disobedience to God's expressed will.

When God gave Adam the precious gift of life He warned him that if he should ever rebel against his Maker the gift would be withdrawn. God was not willing to have an eternal rebellion in His universe. That's why He sent Adam out of the Garden of Eden, away from the tree of life, "lest he put forth his hand, and take also of the tree of life, and eat, and live for ever" (Genesis 3:22).

God should not be blamed for this. He gave Adam life and made provision for him to live forever. It is Satan who was responsible for the tragedy, for he it was who, through Eve, led Adam into disobedience, knowing full well that God couldn't let them both enjoy eternal life once they had transgressed His laws.

That's how death began. It's just as simple as that. Equally easy to understand is the effect that death had on man.

When God gave Adam life He "breathed into his nostrils the breath of life; and man became a living soul" (Genesis 2:7).

The breath of life made that inert body live, transforming it instantly into a living soul. It did not put a separate living soul inside the body.

When Adam died, as ultimately he did, God removed the breath of life from him and he became a *dead* soul. The dust from which he had been created returned "to the earth as it was: and the spirit [or breath]" returned "unto God who gave it" (Ecclesiastes 12:7).

At that instant Adam died, completely and totally. His heart, his muscles, his brain, his memory, everything about him, ceased to function (Ecclesiastes 9:5, 6).

So it is when a person dies today. He does not go on living in some other state, as some people falsely believe. He does not go to heaven or to hell or to purgatory or anywhere else. He merely goes to sleep, as the Bible so gently puts it. Over and over again occurs the phrase, "He slept with his fathers." Exactly. And this sleep will continue until God, in His own good time, brings it to an end in a glad awakening.

So you need never worry that the "soul" of your departed loved one may be enduring fearful torments in some far-off and ill-defined place, and that you must somehow find money enough to get his pains eased. Such pagan fantasies have no Biblical foundation whatever, and no place in Christian teaching.

God has good news for mourners, not frightening stories that only increase their anguish and misery. And this leads to something else you should understand about death.

Adam was God's masterpiece of creation, the most wonderful of all His creatures—a thinking, reasoning, intelligent being, capable of the loftiest, most magnificent achievements. God loved him dearly, as dearly as His own Son, which in a sense he was (Luke 3:38). The last thing God wanted was that this glorious creature should die. So when, because of sin, death became inevitable, God planned *redemption*—a way whereby Adam and his descendants might live again.

To accomplish this, and at the same time keep faith with the rest of His universe, God took the penalty of Adam's sin upon Himself. This was the reason for Bethlehem and Calvary, for Christ's suffering upon the cross and His subsequent resurrection and ascension. All these epochal events were part of the divinely devised plan to give back to man the privilege of living eternally, which God had been compelled to take away from him in the long ago.

It is all clearly summed up in that most beautiful of Bible texts: " 'God loved the world so much that he gave his only Son, that everyone who has faith in him may not die but have eternal life'" (John 3:16, N.E.B.).

This does not mean that everyone is going to be given eternal life. By no means. Everyone *may* have it. Everyone, without exception or discrimination, is included in the plan. It is available to all and free to all. But only those who "have faith in Him" will receive it.

This, of course, is perfectly reasonable. The preservation of His universe being essential, God cannot permit any unrepentant sinner, any hardened rebel against His government, to live forever. He could not allow it in Adam's day and He cannot allow it now.

Those who desire eternal life must be willing to live in harmony with God's commandments, and do those things that please Him—forever. This means they must love Him with all their heart and mind and soul and strength (Matthew 22:37). They must be willing to live like Christ today, tomorrow, always.

People get this way by having "faith in Him"—believing in Him, trusting Him, thinking of Him, talking with Him, acting like Him. Thus they become assured of eternal life. God will never let them out of His sight. He wants them to live with Him always. He would be sad without them, so dear are they to His heart.

When will they receive eternal life? They have it now by promise, but they will receive it in reality at the resurrection when Christ returns to this earth to gather His people to Himself.

He made this very plain when talking to the Jews of His day. " 'In very truth I tell you,' " He said, " 'a time is coming . . . when the dead shall hear the voice of the Son of God, and all who hear shall come to life. . . . The time is coming when all who are in the grave shall hear his voice and move forth: those who have done right will rise to life; those who have done wrong will rise to hear their doom' " (John 5:25-29, N.E.B.).

So the dead will live again. Jesus Christ, Son of the living God, has declared it.

This indeed is the very heart and soul of Christian teaching. Life through Christ is what the gospel is all about.

When Lazarus died and his sister Martha said to Jesus, " 'If you had been here, sir, my brother would not have died,' " Jesus replied, " 'Your brother will rise again.' "

Martha then said, " 'I know that he will rise again at the resurrection on the last day.' Jesus said, 'I am the resurrection and I am life. If a man has faith in me, even though he die, he shall come to life' " (John 11:21-26, N.E.B.).

Then He called Lazarus from the tomb, thereby

demonstrating before all the universe His power over death and His ability to keep His promise to bring all who love Him back from the grave.

A few days later, following His crucifixion, He rose from the dead Himself, making it even more convincingly clear that He is the Lord of life, and making the resurrection of all who love and serve Him an absolute certainty.

Now you can see how great is the good news God has for all who mourn.

If the promise of immortality has become "dim and uncertain" to some, this is no fault of God's. His plans haven't changed. His word remains inviolate. What He has promised He will surely carry out.

In one of His many predictions concerning Christ's first coming, the prophet Isaiah said that He would be anointed "to preach good tidings unto the meek; . . . to bind up the brokenhearted, to proclaim liberty to the captives, and the opening of the prison to them that are bound; . . . to comfort all that mourn" (Isaiah 61:1, 2).

Jesus quoted this passage in His first sermon. See Luke 4:18.

He told His audience that this was exactly what He had come from heaven to do, and in the next three and a half years He did all these things.

He brought good news to the meek.

He bound up the brokenhearted with kind and tender words of sympathy and hope.

He proclaimed liberty to all who were captives of sin, telling them how they might be free.

He told of the opening of the prison house of death and the certain release of all who lay bound in the grave.

And He comforted all who mourned with the glorious good tidings that, if faithful, they would meet their loved ones again.

It was His assurances of life beyond the grave, made so real and forceful by His own dramatic resurrection, that more than anything else brought success to the preaching of the apostles. It was because they were bearers of this great good news that they went forth conquering and to conquer. Such a message was irresistible. Everybody wanted to hear it—everyone who was brokenhearted, everyone who had lost a loved one in death, everyone on the brink of despair.

How the people loved this beautiful message! All their lives they had longed for such good news, and here it was! They could share in it—their very selves, their families. It was almost too good to be true.

But it *was* true. And it *is* true.

Writing to the new church at Corinth the apostle

6

Paul said, "Listen! I will unfold a mystery: we shall not all die, but we shall all be changed in a flash, in the twinkling of an eye, at the last trumpet-call. For the trumpet will sound, and the dead will rise immortal, and we shall be changed. This perishable being must be clothed with the imperishable, and what is mortal must be clothed with immortality. And when our mortality has been clothed with immortality, then the saying of Scripture will come true: 'Death is swallowed up; victory is won!' 'O Death, where is your victory? O Death, where is your sting?' " (1 Corinthians 15:51-55, N.E.B.).

The promise of life through Christ takes the poisonous, soul-destroying sting out of death. It makes the darkened future glow with new hope. It makes despair impossible.

This is what Paul wrote to the church at Thessalonica: "We want you not to remain in ignorance, brothers, about those who sleep in death; you should not grieve like the rest of men, who have no hope. We believe that Jesus died and rose again; and so it will be for those who died as Christians; God will bring them to eternal life with Jesus.

"For this we tell you as the Lord's word: we who are left alive until the Lord comes shall not forestall those who have died; because at the word of command, at the sound of the archangel's voice and God's trumpet-call, the Lord himself will descend from heaven; first the Christian dead will rise, then we who are left alive shall join them, caught up in clouds to meet the Lord in the air. Thus we shall always be with the Lord. Console one another, then, with these words" (1 Thessalonians 4:13-18, N.E.B.).

Here indeed was consolation. Here was a hope which the despairing could grasp and so find new joy in life.

Christ will return. The dead will rise again. The living will meet their loved ones once more. Together they will be "caught up" to meet the Lord. Together they will go to the beautiful dwelling place He has prepared for them. And together they will remain—always, forever and ever.

Here is a beautiful, glorious hope. It is the Christian hope, the blessed hope.

What good news for all who are sad today!

7

No Need to Be Lonely

WHAT A LOT of lonely people there are in the world today! The bereaved and friendless, the neglected and forlorn, the widow, the divorcee, the orphan, disillusioned youth, and children of broken homes. All about us are the thwarted, the frustrated, the unsuccessful, and those who feel that life has passed them by.

With the rapid expansion of cities and the vast increase of apartment houses, the number of lonely people is greater than ever. Partly for self-protection, partly to preserve their isolation, many lock themselves away from would-be friends and neighbors, certain that nobody cares for them and nobody loves them.

Some continue to go about their daily work in office or factory, but with a built-in disappointment or heartbreak, appallingly alone even among many companions. Nothing ever lifts the weight that depresses their spirits.

85

The patriarch Jacob, fleeing from his brother, Esau, with a stone for a pillow, had that wonderful dream of a ladder reaching to heaven, filled with angels.

Maybe you are feeling like this right now. Deserted. Famished for love. Utterly miserable. The most forsaken and neglected person who ever lived. If so, there is good news for you.

If you think that nobody loves you, you are mistaken. Somebody does. God does. And if you will accept His assurances as if they were written especially for you, they will change your outlook on life and put a smile in your eyes again.

"I have loved thee with an everlasting love," He says, "therefore with lovingkindness have I drawn thee" (Jeremiah 31:3).

Although these words were addressed to the people of Israel centuries ago, they apply to you now. God never changes. Nor is He partial. He loves everybody the same. Anyone who wants to be drawn out of his loneliness; anyone who longs to feel encircled with God's lovingkindness; anyone who yearns to experience the deep compassion of His everlasting love may claim this promise for himself.

Equally comforting is King David's assurance that "like as a father pitieth his children, so the Lord pitieth them that fear him."

Kind parents sense immediately when a child needs loving. So does God. He is concerned about every one of us. "For he knoweth our frame; he remembereth that we are dust. As for man, his days are as grass: as a flower of the field, so he flourisheth. For the wind passeth over it, and it is gone; and the place thereof shall know it no more. But the mercy of the Lord is from everlasting to everlasting upon them that fear him, and his righteousness unto children's children; to such as keep his covenant, and to those that remember his commandments to do them" (Psalm 103:13-18).

He remembers each one, thinks of each one, cares for each one, always. From everlasting to everlasting His mercy endures.

In His parable of the Prodigal Son, Christ portrayed God as an infinitely loving Father—a Father with love for the son who ran away and for the son who stayed at home. The boys were very different, but He loved them both the same. His heart followed the runaway clear to the hog pen, and went with the supposedly righteous son to the privacy of his room where no doubt his jealousy first exploded. Both needed love and for both it was provided in abundance.

God loves like a mother, too. "As one whom his mother comforteth," He says, "so will I comfort you" (Isaiah 66:13). Who, at some time or other, has not experienced this exquisitely tender consolation? So full of sympathy and understanding! So patient! So forgiving! So long-suffering!

If a child is lonesome, perchance in the dark, or on a stormy night, or when friends have run away and left him to play alone, how close a mother's arms enfold him! How gentle are her words of consolation!

Toward the lonely, God has most tender thoughts. The Bible says, "He healeth the broken in heart, and bindeth up their wounds. He telleth the number of the stars; he calleth them all by their names. Great is our Lord, and of great power: his understanding is infinite" (Psalm 147:3-5).

This is almost too much to grasp. The God who made the stars, millions upon millions of stars, and placed them in orbit throughout the limitless regions of space, knows each one of them by name. By His power and wisdom He orders their going, directs their paths, sustains them in perpetuity. Yet at the same time He thinks of the humblest of His children, the weakest, the most hurt, the most discouraged. He knows them by name, too. And He heals the broken in heart and binds up their wounds!

How great must be His power, how infinite His understanding!

"O the depth of the riches both of the wisdom and knowledge of God! how unsearchable are his judgments, and his ways past finding out!" (Romans 11:33).

It may be that your loneliness stems from the fact that you have forgotten God, or turned away from Him. Never mind. He loves you still.

"O Israel," He said to His people in the long ago, "return unto the Lord thy God. . . . Take with you words, and turn to the Lord: say unto him, Take away all iniquity, and receive us graciously. . . . For in thee the fatherless findeth mercy" (Hosea 14:1-3).

If they would return—not with money but with words of penitence—then God would "heal their backsliding" and "love them freely." His anger was already "turned away" (verse 4).

Home and friends and companionship await the "fatherless" as they return to God. They await you, too. He isn't angry with you. His love is too great for that.

"Seek ye the Lord while he may be found," He says. "Call ye upon him while he is near: let the wicked forsake his way, and the unrighteous man his thoughts: and let him return unto the Lord, and he will have mercy upon him; and to our God, for he will abundantly pardon" (Isaiah 55:6, 7).

"For the mountains shall depart, and the hills be removed; but my kindness shall not depart from thee" (Isaiah 54:10).

Here once more God assures us of His incredible love—love that outlasts the worst imaginable calamities and reaches out to the loneliest sinner in the most distant and desolate corner of the earth.

In his younger days the patriarch Jacob experienced this pursuing love of God. After twice tricking Esau, robbing him first of his birthright and then of his father's blessing, he fled from home, fearing his brother's revenge. As night came on he began to realize the high cost of his evil course. He had lost his home and his parents and might never see them again. With no place to stay, no friendly lodging where he could rest, he lay down on the bare ground, put his head on a stone, and fell asleep.

Nobody could be as lonely as Jacob was at that moment. Yet he was not alone. Despite his mean, selfish, wicked deeds God had not left him to his own foolish devices. Instead He had followed him to this very spot, still planning how to bring this promising young man back to Him.

As Jacob slept he dreamed. "And behold a ladder set up on the earth, and the top of it reached to heaven: and behold the angels of God ascending and descending on it. And, behold, the Lord stood above it" (Genesis 28: 12, 13).

So there, in that desolate spot, the loneliest place in

the world for him, Jacob found himself face to face with God.

There was that ladder, too, busy as a freeway, with angels coming and going at God's bidding.

How could he feel lonely any more? No wonder when he awoke he cried, "This is none other but the house of God, and this is the gate of heaven" (verse 17).

It was indeed. The gate to a new and happier life.

And what was it that God said to him that night? "Behold, I am with thee, and will keep thee in all places whither thou goest, and will bring thee again into this land; for I will not leave thee, until I have done that which I have spoken to thee of" (verse 15).

It was a promise of divine companionship so that he would never need to feel lonely again. From this night he would live with the assurance of God's constant presence and watchcare.

It was much the same when Moses fled from Egypt. Fearful of Pharaoh's anger, and certain that he was a failure, he trudged on and on into the desert, his heart sinking lower with each labored footstep.

As he approached Sinai there wasn't a human dwelling anywhere, nor a living soul for miles around. But God was there, waiting for him. Out of the burning bush came a voice calling him by name, "Moses, Moses"!

That is what God does. He follows us into our loneliest experiences. He knows exactly when things are at their worst and when we need Him most—and He makes no mistake about our identity. He knows us by name and speaks to us like an old friend.

What He said to Moses He says to each one of us in our darkest, loneliest hours, "Certainly I will be with thee" (Exodus 3:12).

No matter how low and miserable and outcast you may feel, He has good news for you, news that will cheer your heart. Listen to what He said to the forlorn among His people in Isaiah's day:

"Fear not, thou worm Jacob, and ye men of Israel; I will help thee, saith the Lord, and thy redeemer, the Holy One of Israel" (Isaiah 41:14).

God knew how they were feeling. Like a worm. That low. That discouraged. That despised and trodden upon. But He had a remedy.

"Behold," He said, "I will make thee a new sharp threshing instrument having teeth" (verse 15).

Who ever heard of a worm having teeth? Who ever heard of a worm becoming a sharp threshing instrument?

There is a suggestion here of complete and total change—a miraculous transformation of character, vision, purpose—everything.

Note what this transformed worm would do.

"Thou shalt thresh the mountains, and beat them small, and shalt make the hills as chaff" (verse 15).

What a worm! Challenging mountains! Advancing against them with high courage and determination. Sweeping them out of the way!

Nor is this all.

"Thou shalt fan them, and the wind shall carry them away, and the whirlwind shall scatter them" (verse 16).

Who makes this wind? The worm. It has grown wings, powerful wings, with which it creates a gale! Then as it beats its wings with ever-growing fervor the gale becomes a whirlwind and the mountains disappear!

This is what God can do for even a worm—for anyone who feels that low, that lonely, downhearted, and deserted. If you look to Him for help, He will transform you into a person of such courage and power that you will astonish your friends and the world about you.

One thing more. There's something else about this good news you must not miss.

To every promise of His companionship God added a condition—service.

When He said to Moses, "Certainly I will be with thee," He ordered him back to Egypt to deliver Israel from bondage.

When He said to Joshua, "Be strong and of a good courage; be not afraid, neither be thou dismayed: for the Lord thy God is with thee whithersoever thou goest" (Joshua 1:9), He gave him the task of securing Palestine as a permanent home for His people.

When He gave power to the worm to scatter mountains He added this admonition, "Thou shalt rejoice in the Lord, and shalt glory in the Holy One of Israel" (Isaiah 41:16). The worm was not to keep the secret of his miraculous transformation to himself. He must share the glory of it with others.

When He restored the demoniac to full mental health, Christ instructed him, "Return to thine own house, and shew how great things God hath done unto thee" (Luke 8:39).

And when He assured His disciples that He would be with them always, "even unto the end of the world" (Matthew 28:20), He linked this wondrous promise with His last command, "Go ye therefore, and teach all nations, baptizing them in the name of the Father, and of the Son, and of the Holy Ghost: teaching them to observe all things whatsoever I have commanded you" (verse 19).

Here, then, is God's cure for loneliness. First He would have you become aware of His love, His friendship,

His companionship, then go forth to tell other people what a wonderful God and Saviour He is.

Glorifying God as the mountains vanish before you.

Forgetting your own tears as you wipe the tears of others.

Losing your own burdens as you lift the burdens of others.

Finding your life even as you lose it.

And God going with you all the way, from one glad moment to another.

What good news is this!

No Need to Be
So Weary

EVERYBODY SEEMS to be tired. Wherever you go people claim to be worn out and frazzled.

Ask a man how he feels and he is likely to say, "I'd be fine if I weren't so weary." Ask a woman and she will probably answer, "Oh, fine, except I could do with a good sleep."

Despite the gradual reduction of working hours in most trades and businesses, despite the introduction of dozens of labor-saving devices in the home, most people go through life feeling only half alive.

True, they are on the go seven days a week. They drive as fast as the law allows from one activity to another, but they are never really happy because they are forever tired. They keep up the rat race from home to office, from office to home; then from supper to TV program, to bed, and so on—day after day, week after week,

7   97

◂rist here points the children to His great ten-com-
◂andment law given to Moses on two tables of stone
◂ritten by the finger of God at Sinai.

month after month, year after year, hoping that someday there will be time to rest.

But the dream never comes true. The race goes on and on and the hoped-for relaxation never comes—not until it is too late and the overworked body breaks down.

If you are one of those who are forever busy, forever hurried, forever longing for a nap, I have good news for you. You don't need to feel this way.

You may never have thought of it before, but God never intended you or anyone else to live like this. In the beginning He had a much better plan—and still has.

When God created man and placed him in the Garden of Eden, He gave him a program of living with a built-in rest period.

In the second chapter of Genesis, as an integral part of the Creation story, we read: "And on the seventh day God ended his work which he had made; and he rested on the seventh day from all his work which he had made. And God blessed the seventh day, and sanctified it" (Genesis 2:2, 3).

God did not need rest for Himself, of course, for "the everlasting God, the Lord, the Creator of the ends of the earth, fainteth not, neither is weary" (Isaiah 40:28). He ceased His creative activities in order to start man off on a way of life that would be for his perpetual benefit.

As a matter of fact, Adam's first complete day on this earth was a rest day, a Sabbath. He was created on the sixth day, shortly before sunset, and when the sun went down that evening the first Sabbath began.

Adam was introduced to life on this earth on a workless day, a day God had sanctified. In His infinite wisdom and His boundless love for man, He set it apart for the holy purpose of communion with Him.

So Adam began life walking and talking with God. Seven days later he spent another day with God. And so it went on, week after week, an unchanging pattern.

Now, if Adam needed a weekly rest day, how much more do we need one amid this mad rush of the twentieth century! Adam was fresh from his Creator's hands, full of the zest of life, radiant with dynamic energy, free from the effects of disease germs or debilitating habits, with never a trace of weakness from the soles of his feet to the crown of his noble head. Yet God planned that he should rest every seventh day.

With all the ills we have inherited from more than a thousand generations of men and women who have disobeyed God's laws and abused His precious gift of life, with all our proneness to unhealthy habits, we surely stand in far greater need of a weekly rest day than did Adam at the dawn of history.

Adam lived to a great age. The Bible says that he did not die until he was 930 years old. His son, Seth, lived to be 912, and his grandson, Enos, 905. His great-grandson, Cainan, reached 910, his great-great-grandson, Mahalaleel, 895, and his great-great-great-grandson, Jared, 962—and after Enoch, we come to Methuselah, the oldest man who ever lived, who reached 969 years.

Lamech, another of the ancient patriarchs, lived to be 777, and his son, Noah, who rode out the Flood, lived for 950 years.

Many people question these ages as given in the Bible. They say that nobody could have lived that long. But the explanation is simple. All these men lived close to Creation. They knew nothing of the degenerative diseases that are so great a menace today. They ate food grown in mineral-rich, unpolluted soil—food full of life-sustaining elements. More important still, perhaps, was their adherence to the divine plan of a weekly rest day which God ordained in the beginning.

In this connection it should be noted that all except one of the patriarchs mentioned in the fifth chapter of Genesis lived at the same time as Adam. Only Noah never saw him. This means that all of them knew about Creation, for it is inconceivable that Adam would have failed to repeat so thrilling a story over and over again. All of them, therefore, knew about the Garden of Eden. And all of them knew about the seventh-day Sabbath.

Unquestionably, the observance of this rest day had much to do with the length of their lives. They didn't get worn out too soon, as so many do today, by rushing madly from one thing to another seven days a week.

Anyone who spends one day a week resting with God is bound to enjoy better health than those who live day after day, week after week, month after month, with never a thought for God or His gracious provisions for their good.

There's a lot of truth in that old stanza:

"A Sabbath well spent
  Brings a week of content,
  And health for the toils of the morrow;
  But a Sabbath profaned
  Whate'er may be gained
  Is a certain forerunner of sorrow."

There is a basic principle here that is as old as the human race and which goes clear back to Eden.

God made this principle as plain as He could when He gave Moses His Ten Commandments on Mount Sinai.

"Remember the sabbath day, to keep it holy," He said. "Six days shalt thou labour, and do all thy work:

but the seventh day is the sabbath of the Lord thy God: in it thou shalt not do any work, thou, nor thy son, nor thy daughter, thy manservant, nor thy maidservant, nor thy cattle, nor thy stranger that is within thy gates: for in six days the Lord made heaven and earth, the sea, and all that in them is, and rested the seventh day: wherefore the Lord blessed the sabbath day, and hallowed it" (Exodus 20:8-11).

Some have suggested that this was a purely arbitrary, legal requirement of some tyrannical tribal deity. It was nothing of the sort. Instead, it was a gracious provision by the all-wise, all-loving Creator for the well-being of His creatures.

Moses understood it this way. After repeating the Ten Commandments in the fifth chapter of Deuteronomy he wrote: "The Lord commanded us to do all these statutes, to fear the Lord our God, *for our good always, that he might preserve us alive,* as it is at this day" (Deuteronomy 6:24).

As one of the Ten Commandments the Sabbath precept was given "for our good always, that he might preserve us alive." It was something man needed to keep him well and happy. It was a divinely conceived plan to keep him from overwork and from getting so wrapped up in mundane activities that he would forget to develop the spiritual side of his nature. It was part of a well-balanced program to develop the whole man—physical, mental, and spiritual.

Some have expressed the opinion that Christ abolished the Sabbath. That isn't even reasonable. Why should Christ abolish so excellent an arrangement for man's good—a plan He Himself devised?

The New Testament makes it crystal clear that Christ was responsible for the creation of the world and man. The apostle John wrote: "In the beginning was the Word, and the Word was with God, and the Word was God. The same was in the beginning with God. *All things were made by him;* and without him was not any thing made that was made" (John 1:1-3).

Writing to the Colossians about God's "dear Son," the apostle Paul said, "By him were all things created, that are in heaven, and that are in earth, visible and invisible, whether they be thrones, or dominions, or principalities, or powers: *all things were created by him, . . .* and by him all things consist" (Colossians 1:13, 16, 17).

Likewise in the book of Hebrews we read: "God . . . hath in these last days spoken unto us by his Son, whom he hath appointed heir of all things, *by whom also he made the worlds"* (Hebrews 1:1, 2).

Thus it was Christ who created this world, Christ

who made Adam and Eve and placed them in the Garden of Eden, Christ who devised the weekly rest day for their good and to preserve them alive.

The seventh-day Sabbath is therefore Christ's Sabbath, or, as it is more often called, the Christian Sabbath. All who observe it rightly will enjoy the good that Christ planned for those who choose to follow this way of life.

He had more than one reason, of course, for establishing the weekly rest day. For instance, Ezekiel tells us that it was designed to be a sign of allegiance to God. He quotes the Lord as saying, "I gave them my sabbaths, to be a sign between me and them, that they might know that I am the Lord that sanctify them" (Ezekiel 20:12).

Again, "Hallow my sabbaths; and they shall be a sign between me and you, that ye may know that I am the Lord your God" (verse 20).

As people "remember the sabbath day to keep it holy," God remembers them. There is a close bond between them, an identity of spirit and purpose.

By observing every seventh day as God's day, they declare their allegiance to Him before the world, and as they do so, He draws near with many a blessing that others never receive.

This is made clear in Isaiah's counsel to the people of his day: "If thou turn away thy foot from the sabbath, from doing thy pleasure on my holy day; and call the sabbath a delight, the holy of the Lord, honourable; and shalt honour him, not doing thine own ways, nor finding thine own pleasure, nor speaking thine own words: then shalt thou delight thyself in the Lord; and I will cause thee to ride upon the high places of the earth, and feed thee with the heritage of Jacob thy father: for the mouth of the Lord hath spoken it" (Isaiah 58:13, 14).

In this remarkable passage of Scripture the Lord's concern that man should keep the Sabbath day and enjoy its many blessings is clearly evident. Anyone who takes his foot off the Sabbath and remembers that it is God's day will begin to reap rich rewards. He will be blessed physically, mentally, spiritually. He will feel better, think more clearly, and in every way enjoy a far more satisfying life. At one with God, he will taste life's greatest satisfactions and "ride upon the high places of the earth."

So if you are overtired and all tuckered out, there is good news for you. You don't need to feel that way. Follow God's plan for your life and see if it isn't much better than the wretched way you have been living of late.

Next time the seventh day comes around—and you can find which day it is on any calendar—drop everything and rest. Rest for twenty-four hours, from sunset to sunset, as the Bible says. See Leviticus 23:32.

This doesn't mean that you are to go to bed and stay there till the Sabbath is over. But it does mean that you should cease your regular work and your secular pleasures and spend the day with God.

This is what Jesus did, and He should know best how the Sabbath should be observed. He went to church (Luke 4:16); He preached and prayed; and He ministered to the sick.

From the New Testament record it is clear that the Sabbath was often His busiest day. Yet His busy-ness was always in the service of others. And by helping others He Himself was blessed and refreshed for the duties and burdens of the week ahead.

By following His example you will find the way to the help you need. If for one day a week you will forget yourself and remember God, if for this day you will forget your own burdens and think of people more heavily burdened than yourself, if for this day you will forget to seek your own pleasure and try to make others happy, you yourself will be mysteriously refreshed and invigorated. Life will take on new meaning, a new dimension. You will never be so weary again.

9

No Need for So
Much Sickness

THE BIBLE says that when Jesus saw the multitude gathered about Him and so many who "were lame, blind, dumb, maimed, and many others" He had compassion on them (Matthew 15:30-32). All this human misery moved Him deeply.

If He had compassion then, how must He feel today when the numbers of the sick and suffering are ten thousand times as many! Not since the dawn of history have so many people been ill, diseased, maimed, from one cause or another.

In every country on earth crowded hospitals, nursing homes, and clinics tell the sad story. Everywhere there is a shortage of doctors, nurses, and nurse aids to minister to the ever-growing number of patients, a lack that will be greatly accentuated as Medicare and other special types of medical care are adopted around the world.

All this sickness is contrary to God's original plan for the human race, and no doubt He often says, "O that thou hadst hearkened to my commandments! then had thy peace been as a river, and thy righteousness as the waves of the sea" (Isaiah 48:18).

For some types of sickness, of course, the patient cannot be held responsible. Nobody could be blamed for getting cancer, tuberculosis, cerebral palsy, meningitis, Parkinson's disease, or other disorders whose origin is still wrapped in mystery. Nor could anyone be blamed for sickness resulting from an accident or a natural disaster. On the other hand, there are some types of illness that are avoidable, and could be avoided if more care were taken to follow God's counsels on health.

To the Israelites, who had just been freed from Egyptian bondage, God said, "If you will diligently hearken to the voice of the Lord your God, and do that which is right in his eyes, and give heed to his commandments and keep all his statutes, *I will put none of the diseases upon you* which I put upon the Egyptians; for I am the Lord, your healer" (Exodus 15:26, R.S.V.).

This does not mean that God made the Egyptians sick. He didn't. They made themselves sick by the unhealthful things they ate and by the heathen customs they practiced. If Israel would turn away from the bad habits of the

Egyptians, He assured them, they would avoid the diseases from which the Egyptians suffered.

This promise was restated on a later occasion in these words: "I will bless your bread and your water; and *I will take sickness away from the midst of you*" (Exodus 23:25, R.S.V.); but again it was made conditional upon wholehearted loyalty to God which, of course, involved following His good advice on matters concerning their health.

And He *had* good advice for them, excellent advice—advice as good and helpful today as it was when He first gave it to the people of Israel millenniums ago.

And here is more good news for you. It could well be that you could avoid some of the sickness from which you suffer from time to time by paying heed to some of the elementary secrets of good health that have been left on record in the Bible.

This is not saying that the Bible is a medical handbook with detailed diagnoses and cures for every disease; but it certainly contains much wise counsel on how to keep well.

First, it urges *discrimination in diet*.

Thousands of years before medical experts became aware that the food a person eats has a lot to do with his health, God recommended nuts, fruits, and grains as man's best diet. In Genesis 1:29, R.S.V., we read: "And God said, 'Behold, I have given you every plant yielding seed which is upon the face of all the earth, and every tree with seed in its fruit; and you shall have them for food.'"

Had man kept to this original diet he might never have known disease. His only affliction would probably have been the gradual weakening of bodily functions with advancing age.

After the great Flood of Noah's day, when most vegetation was destroyed by that fearful inundation, the eating of animals became customary, and with divine approval. Said God to Noah: "Every moving thing that lives shall be food for you; and as I gave you the green plants, I give you everything. Only you shall not eat flesh with its life, that is, its blood" (Genesis 9:3, 4, R.S.V.).

Note the advice to discriminate. The blood of dead animals was to be avoided. It could be poisonous.

Note also that while God said "I give you everything" the context reveals that He made certain reservations. Some animals were "clean" and others "unclean." This was the basis of their entry into the ark. A certain number of each kind were saved.

The unclean creatures served a useful purpose as scavengers but were unfit for food. A list of such animals, birds, and reptiles is given in the eleventh chapter of Leviticus. It is well worth reading if only to appreciate how sensible is God's counsel on diet discrimination.

Only those animals that part the hoof and are cloven-footed and chew the cud are to be considered clean and therefore edible. All others are unclean and unfit for food. Four are mentioned because of special problems—they meet one but not all three of the specifications—namely, the camel, the rock badger, and the hare—all cud chewers; and the swine which is cloven-footed. "Of their flesh," God says, "you shall not eat" (Leviticus 11:8, R.S.V.).

Concerning fish, the divine recommendation is: "Everything in the waters that has fins and scales, whether in the seas or in the rivers, you may eat. But anything in the seas or the rivers that has not fins and scales . . . is an abomination to you" (verse 9).

As to birds, those prohibited include the eagle, the ossifrage, the osprey, the kite, the falcon, the raven, the ostrich, the nighthawk, the sea gull, the hawk, the owl, the cormorant, the ibis, the water hen, the pelican, the vulture, the stork, the heron, the hoopoe, and the bat, to quote the list given in the Revised Standard Version of Leviticus 11, verses 13-19.

Other creatures listed as unfit for human consumption are the weasel, the mouse, the great lizard, the gecko, the land crocodile, the lizard, the sand lizard, and the chameleon (verses 29, 30).

Who would contest the wisdom of this counsel? Who would want to eat any of these creatures today? Certainly no reputable doctor would recommend them.

Though more than four thousand years old this list is as applicable in 1967 as it was in the days of Moses. God certainly knew what was best.

And this brings into focus His counsel concerning the eating of swine's flesh, the only item on the forbidden list which is widely consumed today under such names as ham, bacon, and other pork products.

What should one do about this? Frankly, the wise course is to drop these items from one's diet. Undoubtedly God had good reason for including the pig with the other scavengers and declaring it unfit to eat. If you agree that the rest of the prohibited list is right and proper—as I am sure you do—why question this one item? Why not accept God's judgment on the matter, remembering that all He plans is for our good always? Dropping this one item from your daily menu could possibly do more for your health than you think.

But this is not all that the Bible has to say on the subject of discrimination in diet. The subject was on the agenda of the first Christian council in Jerusalem. You can read about it in the fifteenth chapter of the book of Acts, where it is recorded that James, the presiding officer, said, "My judgment is that we should not trouble those of the Gentiles who turn to God, but should write to them to abstain from the pollutions of idols and from unchastity and from what is strangled and from blood" (verses 19, 20, R.S.V.).

This counsel was clearly designed to help the early Christians maintain good health; but it was also intended to clarify a problem that had arisen in the church.

At that time many members were more concerned with the religious aspect of diet than with the food itself. The apostle Paul found quite a commotion in some churches over meat offered to idols. Should it or should it not be eaten by Christians? In dealing with this hotly debated subject he outlined some vital principles that all would do well to ponder today.

"Why all this stress on behavior?" he wrote in his letter to the Romans. "Because, as I think you have realized, the present time is of the highest importance—it is time to wake up to reality. Every day brings God's salvation nearer. . . .

"Let us live cleanly, as in the daylight, not in the 'delights' of getting drunk or playing with sex, nor yet in quarreling or jealousies. Let us be Christ's men from head

8

to foot, and give no chances to the flesh to have its fling.

"Welcome a man whose faith is weak, but not with the idea of arguing over his scruples. One man believes that he may eat anything; another man, without this strong conviction, is a vegetarian. The meat eater should not despise the vegetarian, nor should the vegetarian condemn the meat eater—they should reflect that God has accepted them both. After all, who are you to criticize? . . .

"Let us therefore stop turning critical eyes on one another. If we must be critical, let us be critical of our own conduct. . . .

"If your habit of unrestricted diet seriously upsets your brother, you are no longer living in love toward him. And surely you wouldn't let food mean ruin to a man for whom Christ died. . . .

"After all, the kingdom of Heaven is not a matter of whether you get what you like to eat and drink, but of righteousness and peace and joy in the Holy Spirit. . . .

"So let us concentrate on the things which make for harmony, and on the growth of one another's character. Surely we shouldn't wish to undo God's work for the sake of a plate of meat!" (Romans 13:11-20, Phillips).*

Here is a concept of the diet question which was to-

---

* From *The New Testament in Modern English,* © J. B. Phillips 1958. Used by permission of The Macmillan Company.

tally new in Paul's day, yet profound in its insight and meaning. It makes plain that God expects each person to use his own enlightened judgment as to what he eats. After studying what God has revealed concerning the best way to live, and his own basic needs, he is to decide for himself—and his decision is nobody else's business.

Far in advance of its time, this great passage reveals a truth only recently recognized by the medical profession—that no two persons are alike—that each individual has peculiar idiosyncrasies, propensities, allergies, that call for separate, personalized attention.

If and when you become aware of this, you will be able to save yourself much needless suffering. For instance, time after time I noticed that after eating a walnut roast, or other concoction containing these nuts, I would have painful indigestion. Gradually the truth dawned on me that I was allergic to walnuts; that they acted like a poison in my system. Today nobody could persuade me to eat them in any form. In the Pauline fashion I do not judge my friends who consider walnut roasts a rare delicacy, but I see to it that they do not share them with me.

Then there's raw celery. Friends still tell me how good it is; how full of vitamins, et cetera. But it's not for me. So far as my digestive system is concerned it is as poisonous as walnuts. After I quit eating it I was greatly relieved. Then one day, with great caution, I tried some cooked celery, and all was well. Evidently the element in celery to which I am allergic is removed by cooking. I can't explain it, but it is a fact—a fact of life so far as I am concerned. And no matter how many friends urge me to eat raw celery, I don't and I won't.

They may judge me for acting like this, for not eating what they eat, but I am supremely indifferent, comforted by Paul's insistence that every individual must make his own decision as to what kind of food he eats.

And here, I believe, is more good news for you. Learn what is good for you. By trial and error if need be, discover what keeps you in the best health; then make your own decision. You will be surprised how much better you will feel.

But the Bible has more wise counsel on the preservation of health. It recommends that we should *live a balanced life*.

In a previous chapter we considered the vital importance of resting on the seventh day of each week, as recommended in the fourth commandment. Equally important is the mandate, "Six days shalt thou labour."

Rest and work are two inseparable parts of a happy, healthy life. Just as "all work and no play" is harmful, so too is all rest and no work. If you don't have to go to a regular job to earn your livelihood, find something worth while to do, even if you don't get paid for it. There's something highly therapeutic about rendering service to others and living a useful existence. Retired people discovered this long ago. When a person stops making a creative contribution to life he is but a few steps from the hospital or the grave.

The same principle of balance extends into the realm of work and sleep. All too many people think of time spent in sleep as pure waste, and reduce it to a minimum. After a long day of activity they will sit up watching the late TV program, then wonder why they are so tired next morning and have to go around nursing a raging headache. Better far to go to bed at a reasonable time and forgo the program. Ten chances to one it isn't worth looking at anyway.

Here again, as in the matter of diet, all depends upon your personal choice. You can choose to live a sensible, well-balanced life and feel well, or let yourself go, ignore the basic laws of health, and feel sick and miserable. In other words, to a large extent you can choose to be well or sick. That is why Moses, after setting before Israel many important matters, including great health principles, challenged the people to choose aright: "I call heaven and earth to witness against you this day," he said, "that I have set before you life and death, blessing and curse; therefore choose life, that you and your descendants may live, loving the Lord your God, obeying His voice, and cleaving to Him; for that means life to you and length of days" (Deuteronomy 30:19, 20, R.S.V.).

God says this to you today. He wants you to choose life and good health. And I hope you will.

This brings me to the third and perhaps most important of His counsels on health, namely, *avoid damaging your body.*

Despite the gradual deterioration that has taken place over the past six thousand years, the human body is still the most remarkable piece of scientific apparatus in the world. When David said, "I am fearfully and wonderfully made," he uttered a profound truth which medical men are only now beginning to appreciate to the full.

Scientists have designed machines capable of traveling to the moon, but they have never been able to make a man or a woman, and they never will.

They have built the most intricate machines that can add, subtract, multiply, divide, and even remember, but they have never built a computer like the human brain, which can perform all these feats and in addition exercise judgment, manifest compassion, and worship God.

They have built mighty dams and aqueducts, but they

have never produced anything so marvelous as the circulatory system whereby the blood is carried from the heart to the farthermost capillaries, over and over again, without intermission, year after year and decade after decade.

They have spread telegraph and telephone lines around the globe, but have never created a communications system as delicate and accurate as the nervous system, whereby the slightest impressions made upon the eye, the ear, the tongue, the skin, are instantly communicated to the mind and bring forth immediate and appropriate reactions.

They have constructed sewage systems to handle the waste products of the largest cities, but they have never made anything to equal the remarkable process by which wastes are eliminated from the human body.

They have devised the most ingenious ways to feed air to blast furnaces and internal combustion engines, but they have never produced an air-intake system as intricate and perfect as the human lungs.

Only the greatest Scientist of all, the Architect and Creator of the universe, could have devised and produced this miracle of miracles called Man. This explains His concern for the human body and why He pleads so earnestly that it be not harmed.

To the people of Corinth, who were abusing their bodies most tragically, the apostle Paul wrote: "Do you not know that you are God's temple and that God's Spirit dwells in you? If any one destroys God's temple, God will destroy him. For God's temple is holy, and that temple you are" (1 Corinthians 3:16, 17, R.S.V.).

As a matter of fact, God doesn't need to destroy anyone. A person who recklessly damages his body destroys himself.

That is what the Corinthians were doing. Many had let themselves drift into immorality of all kinds. The unpleasant words "adulterers," "homosexuals," and "prostitutes" are all spelled out in the text.

By following this foolish course and misusing the most precious and marvelous of all God's gifts to man, they were not only breaking the seventh commandment of the Decalogue but were inviting endless sickness and pain. In very truth they were destroying themselves.

"Shun immorality," the apostle urged them. "Every other sin which a man commits is outside the body; but the immoral man sins against his own body" (1 Corinthians 6:18, R.S.V.).

Then he asked again, "Do you not know that your body is a temple of the Holy Spirit within you, which you have from God? You are not your own; you were bought with a price. So glorify God in your body" (verses 19, 20).

These basic principles apply with equal force to other ways whereby people abuse and damage their bodies. Smoking tobacco, for instance. Drinking alcoholic beverages. Taking narcotic drugs.

I don't need to produce evidence to prove that all these practices are harmful. It is common knowledge. The facts have been published in every newspaper, in the *Reader's Digest,* the *Saturday Evening Post,* and hundreds of other journals.

Six million alcoholics in the United States alone should be proof enough of the harm done by alcohol.

Tens of thousands of deaths from lung cancer are surely sufficient evidence of the perils of smoking. And the Surgeon General's report on the subject should be sufficient to convince any reasonable person. Furthermore, Congress has ordered cigarette manufacturers to print a warning notice on every package.

As for the misuse of drugs, nobody attempts to defend this ugly, mind-destroying practice.

All these habits result from personal choice. If you are involved in any one of them, here is an area in which you can decide for yourself whether you want to be sick or well. You can let things go on as they are and take the consequences or you can put your foot down and say, "I won't do this foolish thing any longer"—a decision that will immediately set you on the high road to health and happiness.

This is why I say that there is no need for so much sickness. Concerning some afflictions you cannot do anything. If you have lost a finger or a toe or a kidney, you can't put it back again. But in regard to what you eat and drink or smoke—to what you deliberately put in your mouth—you can do much. Here the choice is yours.

You can choose health, strength, and vigor or sickness, weakness, and misery.

If you say, "I'd like to feel strong and well again, but I simply can't give up my cigarettes, my cocktails, my coffee, my bacon, my tasty but indigestible foods," that's something else again. In this case I suggest you turn to the next chapter where you will find still more good news for you.

10

You Can Overcome!

EVERYBODY IS familiar with the so-called civil rights song "We Shall Overcome Someday." Its haunting melody floats into every home over radio and TV almost every day, reminding us all that some very sincere people are determined to get something they have wanted desperately for a long, long time.

The general idea, of course, came out of the Bible, which has much to say about overcoming. In the book of Revelation two chapters are devoted to the subject and seven promises are made to the overcomer.

1. "To him that overcometh will I give to eat of the tree of life" (Revelation 2:7).

2. "He that overcometh shall not be hurt of the second death" (verse 11).

3. "To him that overcometh will I give to eat of the hidden manna" (verse 17).

4. "He that overcometh, . . . to him will I give power over the nations" (verse 26).

5. "He that overcometh, the same shall be clothed in white raiment" (chapter 3:5).

6. "Him that overcometh will I make a pillar in the temple of my God" (verse 12).

7. "To him that overcometh will I grant to sit with me in my throne" (verse 21).

These promises, rich in symbolism, indicate how much importance God places on overcoming. Not *collective* overcoming, as in a war or a political campaign, but *personal* overcoming in the daily struggle with evil.

It is worth noting that the Greek word rendered "overcome" in the King James Version appears as "conquer" in the Revised Standard Version and "victorious" in the *New English Bible*. Likewise the Berkeley Version speaks of "the victor" and Moffatt's translation of "the conqueror."

There is an old saying that "the conqueror takes the spoils," and this is as true in spiritual as in secular matters. Those who overcome harmful habits and evil temptations reap rich blessings in this life as well as in the life to come.

Of special encouragement is the assurance that it *is possible* to overcome. There is no need to give in to

Amid the most sordid circumstances, when indulgence in sinful pleasure holds sway over heart and will, Christ often pleads with youth to forsake evil.

any temptation or to consider any bad habit impossible to shake off. With God's help, victory over the worst habits can be achieved. There are no shackles so strong that they cannot be broken.

Here is more good news for you. Great good news.

I don't know what habit you are trying to break, but take courage! You can overcome.

Remember that you are not the only one engaged in a struggle of this sort. Millions are fighting a similar battle. Some are battling the drink habit, others the smoking habit, others the drug habit. Still others are struggling against a variety of harmful indulgences, including the temptation to overeat.

Early in 1965 a group of Seventh-day Adventists living in Seattle decided to seek out people who might be needing help in this type of warfare. As a first step they inserted an advertisement in a newspaper, which ran like this: "If you want to overcome the smoking habit, call————," the number being that of the Adventist church.

Within the next twenty-four hours 42,000 calls were received. Busy signals backed up until the whole telephone system of north Seattle was clogged. Officials of the telephone company begged that the experiment be stopped.

Since then a similar notice has been placed in other newspapers in various cities, with similar results. Invariably the telephone line becomes jammed with calls. In the Bay Area, south of San Francisco, five lines had to be installed to handle the traffic, and these were used to capacity for several days.

These experiments have revealed how widespread is the yearning to break the tobacco habit. They suggest that there must be hundreds of thousands of people who recognize they are slaves to it, know it is harmful, and are willing to do almost anything to get free of it.

What happens to the people who respond to the advertisement?

Wherever possible they are introduced to what has become known around the world as the Five-Day Plan to Stop Smoking, devised some years ago by Elman Folkenberg and Dr. Wayne McFarland. Operated as a service to humanity, and entirely free of charge, this plan is simplicity itself, appealing instantly to the common sense of all who take part in it. In most cases it is conducted by a doctor and a minister who between them present the sober facts concerning (1) the harmful effects of tobacco on the human system, and (2) ways and means whereby the craving for tobacco can be eliminated.

During the past few years the results of the Five-Day

Plan have been remarkable. In many cases more than 50 per cent of those attending the instruction classes have obtained total victory over the smoking habit, with another 25 per cent reducing their use of cigarettes substantially.

If you are interested in the plan, and would like more details on how it works, the publishers of *Good News for You* will be glad to send you the information.

Regarding the use of alcoholic beverages, there are as many people eager to quit this body-destroying practice as there are who want to overcome the smoking habit.

In this matter also Seventh-day Adventists are out in front with plans to help people find deliverance. Being nondrinkers and nonsmokers themselves, they are in a peculiarly advantageous position to render assistance.

They have initiated a School for Alcoholic Studies, where the dangers of alcohol are discussed by prominent community leaders. They have established a worldwide chain of temperance societies whose purpose is to discourage the use of alcohol and help those who have become addicted to it. *Listen,* their first-class monthly magazine, dedicated to presenting the facts about alcohol and tobacco to youth, is the only periodical of its kind in the world.

Alcoholics Anonymous is another organization designed to help those who know alcohol is harming them and are eager to free themselves from its shackles. Its number is to be found in most telephone books. There is no longer need for anyone to be a slave to this habit. Help is only a telephone call away.

Whether a person obtains freedom from a harmful habit depends to a large degree on how much he wants that freedom.

The person who says "I'll cut my tobacco quota down to one pack a day" will never overcome the smoking habit.

Likewise the one who says "I'll reduce my whisky consumption to a bottle a week" will never overcome the drinking habit.

If you want to overcome smoking or drinking or any other harmful habit, it will have to be all or nothing on your part. You must *want* deliverance sincerely, even desperately. No mere wish is sufficient to win in so great a struggle.

You will also need the help of God, and you should ask Him earnestly for it; but God won't help you conquer the smoking habit if you want to go on smoking. Nor will He help you break the drinking habit if you want to continue taking alcohol. Your desire and purpose are intimately linked with God's intervention. If God sees that you are sincere, that you have made up your mind to be free, His help will be forthcoming instantly.

It was on this basis that some of Christ's greatest miracles were wrought.

On one occasion a father brought his sick son to Him and pleaded for help. As the boy went into convulsions and "rolled about foaming at the mouth," Jesus asked the father, " 'How long has he been like this?'

" 'From childhood,' " the father replied, going on to explain that often the boy had fallen into the fire or water. Then, revealing how deeply concerned he was for his son, he said, " 'If it is at all possible for you, take pity upon us and help us.'

" 'If it is possible!' said Jesus. 'Everything is possible to one who has faith.'

" 'I have faith,' cried the boy's father; 'help me where faith falls short.' " See Mark 9:14-25, N.E.B.

The boy was healed instantly. Why? First, because the father wanted help so desperately, and second, because he believed Jesus had power to heal.

On another occasion two blind men approached Jesus requesting the restoration of their sight. Following Him, they cried out, " 'Son of David, have pity on us!' "

Jesus stopped and said to them, " 'Do you believe that I have the power to do what you want?'

" 'Yes, sir,' " they said with great eagerness.

"Then he touched their eyes, and said, 'As you have

believed, so let it be'; and their sight was restored" (Matthew 9:27-29, N.E.B.).

Note again how a deep yearning for deliverance was linked to the healing power of God.

Then there was the woman who for twelve years had been troubled with internal bleeding. She had gone to all the doctors she knew and spent all her savings in vain. Her longing for help was very real and she showed it by pressing through the crowd and touching Jesus' cloak, saying to herself, " 'If I touch even his clothes, I shall be cured' " (Mark 5:28, N.E.B.).

As the bleeding stopped, Jesus turned to the woman and said, " 'My daughter, your faith has cured you. Go in peace, free for ever from this trouble' " (verse 34).

In this case a great yearning plus great faith wrought a complete and permanent cure.

When the disciples asked Jesus why they had been unable to help the father with the sick son, He made it plain that it was because they didn't care enough. They weren't sufficiently concerned. " 'Your faith is too weak,' " He said, adding, " 'I tell you this: if you have faith no bigger even than a mustard-seed, you will say to this mountain, "Move from here to there!", and it will move; nothing will prove impossible for you' " (Matthew 17:20, N.E.B.).

Move a mountain? Yes, indeed. Any "mountain"—if you *want* it moved sufficiently, and if you believe God can help you move it.

On another occasion, when the disciples asked Jesus to increase their faith, He replied, " 'If you had faith no bigger even than a mustard-seed, you could say to this sycamore-tree, "Be rooted up and replanted in the sea"; and it would at once obey you' " (Luke 17:6, N.E.B.).

Obviously He was using symbolic language, for who would ever want to transplant a sycamore tree, or any other tree, in the sea? Once more He was trying to convey the great truth that if they wanted something earnestly enough, and believed God had power enough to make it happen, it would happen.

The apostle Paul followed this basic principle with startling results. Arriving at Lystra on one of his missionary journeys through Asia Minor, he came across "a crippled man, lame from birth, who had never walked in his life" (Acts 14:8, N.E.B.). Looking him in the face, Paul "saw that he had the faith to be cured" and told him to stand up. At this the man "sprang up and started to walk" (verse 10).

What did Paul see in this man's face? Eagerness, a desperate longing to be able to walk, plus belief that Paul could help him. The two combined were irresistible.

If God sees such a look on *your* face, you will have no trouble breaking any harmful habit that may have taken a grip on your life. When your yearning for deliverance meets His longing to help you, the problem will be solved in no time at all.

Paul told the Romans, "Overwhelming victory is ours through him who loved us" (Romans 8:37, N.E.B.).

That's true. That's the sort of victory He has in mind for you. Not a partial and temporary one, but total, permanent, and overwhelming.

A preacher friend of mine has a most unusual necklace which he wears on certain occasions. It is composed of dozens of pipes—smokers' pipes—that have been given him over the years by men who have overcome the tobacco habit. Each one speaks of a personal triumph, but together they shout the praises of God who gave overwhelming victory to so many.

If you want deliverance from the smoking habit, the drinking habit, or any other habit that is holding you in slavery and making you less of a man, less of a woman, than you know God wants you to be, *you can have it.*

You *can* be free. You *can* be victorious. You *can* overcome. Not "someday," as the song says, but now.

11

You Can Fortify
Your Faith

FOLLOWING THEIR victory over the central powers in 1918, the Allies scrapped their tanks, destroyed their planes, sank a considerable part of their navies, all in the mistaken belief that there never would be another war.

Twenty years later they discovered how wrong they had been. When World War II exploded they found themselves almost totally unprepared. While they had lulled themselves to sleep with the old and deadly ditty "Peace, peace"—when there was no peace—the enemy had regained his strength, rearmed, and was ready to fight again.

In 1945 the same process was repeated. No sooner had Germany and Japan been defeated than talk of disarmament began again, and the United Nations organization was set up in the hope of making another

135

Young people whose faith is founded on the Word of God are furnished with the best possible defense against the corruption and defilement of the world.

war impossible. It didn't work. New enemies with new weapons appeared, and today a worse conflict seems inevitable. In this wicked world letting down one's guard is now recognized to be a very poor policy.

In the same wicked world the Christian has to learn a similar lesson. Conquering one bad habit is not enough. Overcoming must be a continuing experience. One victory is not enough. One has to be constantly ready to meet and vanquish temptation. To be safe one needs to keep his spiritual armor forever in first-class condition and grow in spiritual strength from day to day.

Is this possible? It is indeed. You *can* fortify your faith and make the fortress of your soul impregnable.

Here is the good news as the apostle Paul colorfully expressed it: "Find your strength in the Lord, in his mighty power. Put on all the armour which God provides, so that you may be able to stand firm against the devices of the devil. For our fight is not against human foes, but against cosmic powers, against the authorities and potentates of this dark world, against the superhuman forces of evil in the heavens.

"Therefore, take up God's armour; then you will be able to stand your ground when things are at their worst, to complete every task and still to stand.

"Stand firm, I say. Buckle on the belt of truth; for

coat of mail put on integrity; let the shoes on your feet be the gospel of peace, to give you firm footing; and, with all these, take up the great shield of faith, with which you will be able to quench all the flaming arrows of the evil one. Take salvation for helmet; for sword, take that which the Spirit gives you—*the words that come from God*" (Ephesians 6:10-17, N.E.B.).

This picturesque prose has a suggestion for us of vital importance. God has made provision for our faith to be so strengthened that no matter who or what our enemies may be, nor how powerful and seductive they may be, we can be victorious over them. Even cosmic forces and superhuman forces of evil in the heavens—surely the ultimate in the opposition we may face—cannot prevail against the man or woman who has donned the divine armor. "The words that come from God" will make him invincible.

The apostle Peter expressed the same truth in his second letter to the Christians of his day.

"Grace and peace be yours in fullest measure, through the knowledge of God and Jesus our Lord," he said to them.

"His divine power has bestowed on us everything that makes for life and true religion, enabling us to know the One who called us by his own splendour and might.

Through this might and splendour *he has given us his promises*, great beyond all price, *and through them you may escape the corruption with which lust has infected the world,* and come to share in the very being of God.

"With all this in view, you should try your hardest to supplement your faith with virtue, virtue with knowledge, knowledge with self-control, self-control with fortitude, fortitude with piety, piety with brotherly kindness, and brotherly kindness with love" (2 Peter 1:2-7, N.E.B.).

Note again that it is "the words that come from God," in the form of "his promises," that provide divine protection and enable a person "to escape the corruption with which lust has infected the world." By reading these Heaven-inspired words, memorizing them, and endeavoring to recall them in every time of need, a person will develop a character strong enough to meet any foe or any emergency. He will "grow in grace, and in the knowledge of our Lord and Saviour Jesus Christ" (2 Peter 3:18), being mightily fortified thereby.

Where may one find "the words that come from God" —the potent words that can enable a person to confront all evil triumphantly and stand his ground "when things are at their worst, to complete every task and still to stand"?

In the Bible, of course. Where else?

If you want to fortify your faith you must spend time with this Book. If you want "overwhelming victory" to be your constant experience you must make Bible study part of your life.

Many are weak, unable to stand against the simplest temptation, because they never open the Bible. They say they aren't interested or they haven't time, though they have time for everything else they want to do. They would rather read the newspaper or look at a TV program. As a result they fail to receive the help they need to battle successfully with the subtle and powerful evils of these latter days.

Should you perchance be one of those who have never sensed the power of "the words that come from God," maybe the trouble lies in the way you have regarded the Bible, or possibly the way you have approached it. All too many look upon it as a bore. Others think of it as some sort of talisman, or book of magic, to provide immediate answers to specific problems. So they flip the pages backward and forward, looking for some striking passage to meet their need. When they land in the middle of the genealogies of the Chronicles or the wheels and wings of Ezekiel or the "begats" of Matthew one, they slam it shut in disappointment and disgust.

That's no way to read so wonderful a volume. There is a better way. Here are eight suggestions summarized briefly from my book *How to Read the Bible,* which you may find helpful. Follow them and I believe you will come to agree with me that the Bible is the most fascinating Book you ever read.

1. Begin with one of the simplest books, such as the Gospel of Mark. Read it through. It won't take long, not more than an hour at the most.

Here is the earliest record of the life and death of Jesus Christ, as told by eyewitnesses to John Mark. You will find it very easy reading. It will introduce you not only to the New Testament but also to the basic facts of the Christian faith.

2. Next read the Gospel of Matthew. This book was written several years later than Mark's and repeats almost every line of it. In addition, however, it gives many of the teachings of Jesus that Mark omitted.

Matthew reports six of the sermons of Jesus, the first and most familiar being the Sermon on the Mount. In this are found the Beatitudes, the golden rule, and the Lord's Prayer.

3. After Matthew, read the Gospel written by Luke, whose interest in medical matters gave him a humanitarian outlook and led him to record the parables of the

Good Samaritan, the Prodigal Son, and the Rich Man and Lazarus.

4. Now read the Gospel of John, which was written at least thirty years after the other three. During this time the Christian church had become established, and John recorded his most treasured memories of Jesus for its encouragement.

When you have read the four Gospels you will have had the finest possible introduction to the Bible. You will be prepared to go forward to the book of Acts to read Luke's story of the growth of the early church; or, if you prefer, turn back to Genesis to find the beginning of the tragedy of sin, which ultimately caused Christ's death.

5. Look for the stories in the Bible. There are hundreds. If you happen to possess the ten-volume set of *The Bible Story* you will find 409 stories listed in the index.

6. Search for God's promises. They are legion, covering almost every aspect of life and every human need. Memorize some of them for future use.

7. Pick out the biographies. The Bible is full of them. Unlike many books of biography, it tells the bad as well as the good points of its various characters.

You will enjoy the life of David. From the moment he steps on the Bible stage as an innocent shepherd lad to his last stirring oration as the dying king of Israel, his story will grip your heart. Incidentally, his is the longest biography in the Old Testament, covering about one thirteenth of the whole. You will find most of it in 1 Samuel, chapters 16 to 31, all of 2 Samuel, and the first and second chapters of 1 Kings.

In the New Testament the most notable biography, apart from the story of Jesus and occasional glimpses of His disciples, is that of Paul. He steps on the scene in Acts 7:58 as an official of the Sanhedrin at the stoning of Stephen, moves to the center of the stage in chapter 9, and stays there through most of the remainder of the book. His three missionary journeys are described in much detail as he strives to bring the story of Christ to Jerusalem, Damascus, Antioch, Tarsus, Athens, Corinth, Philippi, Ephesus, and finally to Rome. He was the great city evangelist of the first century A.D., with a story you should not fail to read.

8. Think of the Bible as a library in which to pursue a variety of studies. With the aid of a concordance, or a reference Bible, you will be able to choose any one of hundreds of subjects and find out what the Bible has to say about it.

Don't try to read too much at one time. Take it easy. Relax. Bible reading is not a race or an endurance trial.

Nor is there any special virtue in reading it through in so many hours, days, or weeks. Rapid scanning won't help you very much.

The Bible is a book for meditation. Far better read one chapter slowly, thoughtfully, prayerfully, than a whole book in a wild hurry to reach the last verse or accomplish some predetermined program.

Take time to enjoy it. Try to think what the words really mean. Roll the lovely phrases around in your mind. You will be surprised how beautiful they will become.

Frequently I have spent hours of concentrated thought on a few brief verses, and how very rewarding it has always been! This is when the Bible glows. When at length you put it down you have a feeling that you have been in the very presence of God.

Glorious thoughts come leaping up from seemingly dry and meaningless words like snowdrops bursting from the barren earth in the spring. Passages to which you have never before given much attention become like harp strings upon which angels play the melodies of heaven.

As you continue to study the Bible you will become more and more convinced that it is indeed the Word of God. You will also discover the strongest proof of its inspiration—*it inspires those who read it.*

Make a habit of reading this unique Book. Seek earnestly for its hidden treasures. Try to read at least a few verses every day.

As your interest grows, enroll in a reliable Bible correspondence course. Some of the best courses are offered by the Voice of Prophecy radio program, Box 55, Los Angeles, California 90053. Another valuable course is conducted by the well-known TV program Faith for Today, Box 8, New York, N.Y. 10008.

When you have taken one of these courses, don't rest content. Send for another. You can never study the Bible too much.

As you study—and make use of what you study—you will find yourself becoming "mighty in the Scriptures." In "the words that come from God" you will discover power to live a noble, virtuous life. They will become your secret armor. They will help you overcome.

Thus will your faith be fortified, enabling you to gain victory after victory over all "the devices of the devil." With the apostle Paul you will be able to say, "Wherever I go, thank God, he makes my life a constant pageant of triumph in Christ" (2 Corinthians 5:14, Moffatt).

You Can Talk
to God

WHILE VISITING New Zealand not long ago I chanced to meet Vera—a little girl of eight who had quite a story to tell me.

She once lost three or four teeth in an accident and a dentist replaced them with a tiny plate. Next day, as she played on the beach, a big wave knocked her down. When she got to her feet the precious plate was gone. She searched everywhere for it. So did her friends. But they couldn't find it.

When her parents rebuked her for being so careless she replied, "Don't worry. I've asked God to help me find it, and He will."

Her mother told her it wasn't right to pray about something like this, and her father said it was foolish to expect to find a tiny plate like hers in the ocean, especially when it looked like a piece of broken seashell.

But Vera kept on praying.

When the tide went out dozens of boys and girls came to help, tramping all over the sand and making the plate even harder to find. At last Vera's parents decided it was time to go home to eat. They were gone several hours. When they returned the tide was back in.

By this time everybody had given up hope of ever seeing that plate again—everybody, that is, except Vera. Once more she started walking up and down in the water, looking this way and that and praying as she looked.

"Please, dear God," she kept saying, "send me back my little plate."

Then it was that another big wave came rolling in— just like the one that had knocked her over. As it crashed on the sand she saw a tiny white thing being pushed relentlessly up the beach, finally coming to rest right between her feet. It was her little plate!

Rushing to her parents, she cried, "Look! God has sent it back to me. I knew He would, and He did."

She was all aglow as she told me the story. I checked it carefully with her mother, who assured me that it was absolutely true.

God was very real to that child, and still is. She talks to Him and is certain that He answers her. The greatest theologians in the world couldn't persuade her otherwise.

Jane was on vacation in Florida with her family. They were camping by a river and ate their meals on the bank. One day after lunch, when it was Jane's turn to clear away the paper dishes and napkins, instead of burning them as she should have done, she threw them into the river. As the last of the place mats went sailing out across the water she gave a cry of alarm. Her precious white-gold watch had gone too!

Her cry brought all the family to the riverbank, but there was nothing anyone could do about it.

"I'm afraid it's gone for good," said her mother. "Nobody could find a watch out there. The water's too deep."

"But let's try!" cried Jane. "I've asked God to help me find it and I'm sure He will. Can't we take the boat out?"

They took the boat out and as it drifted downstream Jane peered into the water as best she could and scanned every inch of the bank, praying earnestly as she searched.

They must have traveled a mile or more and were about to give up when Jane spotted one of the paper napkins she had thrown away. It was snagged in the branches of a fallen tree. As the boat glided by she cried, "Look! My watch! It's floating on the napkin!"

It was indeed, and all the angels in heaven must have rejoiced at the glow of gladness and gratitude on her face at that moment.

PAINTING BY HARRY BAERG   © 1966 BY REVIEW AND HERALD →

The terrible brush fire was licking up everything in its path. Jennifer dropped to her knees and cried, "Please, God, make the sheep go through the gate!"

A million-to-one accident? Who can tell? For myself I prefer to believe that Jane, like so many other children, had a clear line to the heart of God; and in His infinite wisdom and power He knew exactly how to help her.

Jennifer lives on a sheep ranch in South Australia. One day not long ago news came that a grass fire was advancing swiftly toward her home. Her father ran for the hose and started drenching the house with water, at the same time sending ten-year-old Jennifer with two dogs to bring in the sheep.

To get the sheep into the corral near the house meant driving them through a narrow gate, but they refused to

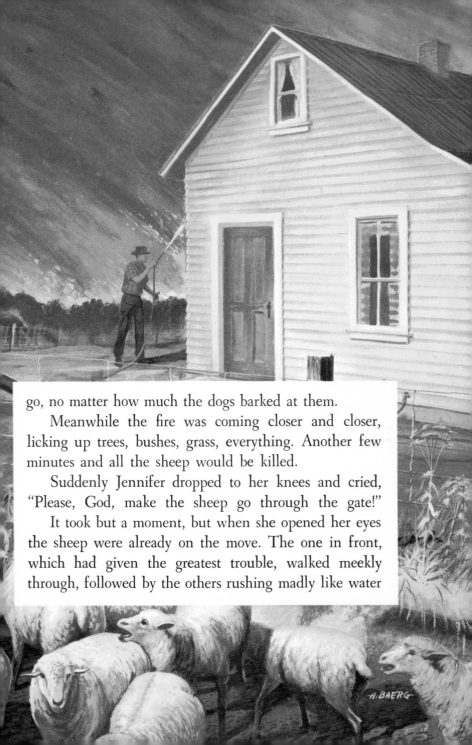

go, no matter how much the dogs barked at them.

Meanwhile the fire was coming closer and closer, licking up trees, bushes, grass, everything. Another few minutes and all the sheep would be killed.

Suddenly Jennifer dropped to her knees and cried, "Please, God, make the sheep go through the gate!"

It took but a moment, but when she opened her eyes the sheep were already on the move. The one in front, which had given the greatest trouble, walked meekly through, followed by the others rushing madly like water through a broken dam. Soon they were all in the corral near the house and safe from the fire. Jennifer will always believe God answered her prayer in that moment of desperate need.

Some time after World War II broke out a boy and a girl living in Devonshire, England, each began to pray for a banana. They hadn't tasted one for months because the import of bananas was prohibited as being nonessential to the war effort. The children did not understand this and were certain that God could and would send them one. In vain did their mother explain why they should not pray such a prayer. They prayed on.

Then one day a banana arrived. Just one. It came wrapped in a shoebox—a present from a friend of the family who had brought a few bananas into the country in his personal baggage.

At first the children were thrilled. Their prayer had been answered! Then their faces fell. Something was wrong. When their mother inquired the cause of their disappointment they explained, "We asked for one each and He has only sent one!"

Then an amazing thing happened. As their mother peeled off the skin she exclaimed, "Look, children! There *are* two. It's a twin banana. He has sent you one each after all!"

Those children never forgot that extraordinary answer to their prayer. They grew up with God, ever thinking of Him as their special Friend. Today the boy is a minister of the gospel, and the girl is married to a minister.

For more than forty years I have been collecting similar stories about children's prayers and the wonderful ways God has answered them. You will find scores of them in my *Uncle Arthur's Bedtime Stories*. Together they bear powerful testimony to the fact that children, in some mysterious way, *do* get through to God. Somehow their simple, unquestioning faith leaps all barriers, and touching the heart of infinite Love, brings swift answers to their petitions. There may be much more truth than we have thought in the oft-quoted words of Jesus, "Unless you turn round and become like children, you will never enter the kingdom of Heaven" (Matthew 18:3, N.E.B.).

Children know the way to the kingdom and have no doubt about it.

The pity is that as they grow up and go to school, all too often they come under the influence of atheistic teachers and lose their intimate relationship with God. Gradually He fades out of their lives. But while *they* change, God does not. Nor does He forget them. He loves them still, hoping that someday they will talk to Him again as they did in years gone by.

He wants *you* to talk to Him as you once did when you were a child. No matter what may have happened in the meantime, you are still most dear to Him. Nothing would please Him more than to hear your voice again. Tenderly He says to you, as He said to the people of Isaiah's day, "Come now, and let us reason together . . . : though your sins be as scarlet, they shall be as white as snow" (Isaiah 1:18).

If you can bring yourself to do this, you will be greatly blessed. Prayer—which is but another word for talking to God—will bring you into touch with the Infinite, the Omnipotent, the Eternal. It will link you with the Source of all good, all wisdom, and all life. It will put you instantly on the "hot" line to Heaven and give you access to the richest treasures of the universe.

This is great good news. For it is wonderful beyond words that you and I—anyone on earth—can talk to so great and good a Friend any time, anywhere.

Breathtaking are the promises of God to those who communicate with Him. They suggest that He wants us to talk to Him far more eagerly than we ever supposed.

"They that seek the Lord shall not want any good thing," He says (Psalm 34:10).

Again: "Delight thyself also in the Lord; and he shall give thee the desires of thine heart" (Psalm 37:4).

"The Lord shall open unto thee his good treasure," Moses assured the children of Israel (Deuteronomy 28: 12), which was like saying, "If there is anything you want, come and take it." This is equivalent to a blank check on the bank of Heaven. It awaits only our personal endorsement.

Nor was this promise restricted to the children of Abraham. God is equally generous to all who love and obey Him today.

When Jesus came to reveal God to man He confirmed all these Old Testament promises, adding some even more generous.

To His disciples He said, " 'If you ask anything in my name I will do it' " (John 14:14, N.E.B.). Again, " 'If you dwell in me, and my words dwell in you, ask what you will, and you shall have it' " (John 15:7, N.E.B.).

If words mean anything, it would seem that God has made provision for every holy desire to be granted. If we "have not" it is because we "ask not" (James 4:2).

Through Christ He seeks to enrich our lives in every possible way. "You know how generous our Lord Jesus Christ has been," wrote the apostle Paul. "He was rich, yet for your sake he became poor, so that through his poverty you might become rich" (2 Corinthians 8:9, N.E.B.).

God's benevolence is limitless. It covers every conceivable need you may have. If you lack wisdom or faith or courage or the essentials of life, you are to talk to Him about it. Make your needs known—He will supply them.

Talking to God will also help you understand Him better and love Him more. It will also open up to you the hidden glories of the Bible as you have never seen them before. Prayer and Bible study should go together. The Bible is God's Book, and what could be more reasonable than to ask His help to appreciate it more fully?

It is God's special joy to do great things for His children and He is well able "to do exceeding abundantly above all that we ask or think" (Ephesians 3:20).

In the *New English Bible* this verse says that He "is able to do *immeasurably more* than all we can ask or conceive."

Immeasurably more! What an offer! Why not make the most of it?

It is the same offer that God made to Jeremiah centuries ago. "Call unto me," He said, "and I will answer thee, and shew thee great and mighty things, which thou knowest not" (Jeremiah 33:3).

Here is another invitation to us to talk to God, coupled with a promise of unlimited assistance. It resembles this beautiful promise: "Before they call, I will answer; and while they are yet speaking, I will hear" (Isaiah 65:24).

To support these divine assurances the Bible provides one example after another of swiftly answered prayers. It tells how Elijah, confronting a menacing crowd, cried out to God, "Let it be known this day that thou art God in Israel, and that I am thy servant, and that I have done all these things at thy word" (1 Kings 18:36). God heard his cry and moments later "the fire of the Lord fell."

It tells how Hezekiah, threatened by the king of Assyria, took his burden to the Lord. "Incline thine ear, O Lord, and hear," he cried; "open thine eyes, O Lord, and see; and hear all the words of Sennacherib. . . . O Lord our God, save us from his hand" (Isaiah 37:17-20).

That very night the Assyrian army was mysteriously destroyed, and Sennacherib returned to Nineveh without so much as shooting an arrow at Jerusalem.

The Bible tells how Jeremiah, crying for help from the bottom of a slimy pit, looked up to see a friendly Ethiopian come to set him free (Jeremiah 38:12, 13).

To all these people, God was very personal. They asked for His help and received it.

As the Negro spiritual says, "The God who lived in Daniel's day is just the same today." He is. He helps men, women, and children in the twentieth century A.D. the same as He helped people for thousands of years B.C.

During World War II, when millions found themselves for the first time face to face with desperate danger, many turned to God for help and found Him a wonder-working Friend. Unforgettable are the stories of Lieutenant Whittaker and his companions who while on a life raft in the Pacific prayed for water and saw a rain cloud come to them against the wind; of Major Allen Lindberg who in similar tragic plight prayed for deliverance and was providentially found by heathen tribesmen; of John Kennedy's rescue in the Solomon Islands by Methodist and Seventh-day Adventist natives.

Shortly after the war, Chaplain W. C. Taggart wrote:

"I know of men lost and starving in the deserts of Australia who were found and brought to safety after asking God for help. Of men in bombers shot to pieces by enemy gunfire who, quite literally, prayed their way back to base. I know, too, that many times appeals uttered by mothers, wives, and sweethearts in the United States stretched a protective mantle half around the globe to shield us in the South Pacific.

"One high-ranking general told me that he owes his life, in part, to the petitions voiced by his closest friend and former business partner. I myself am living on borrowed time because my parents prayed for me in a situation of great danger."

Not every prayer is answered, and with good reason. In our inexperience we sometimes ask for things which if granted would be harmful to us. Knowing this, God doesn't give them to us. Consequently, we should always say, as Jesus did in Gethsemane, "Thy will be done" (Matthew 26:42). Only as we ask "according to his will" does He answer us (1 John 5:14).

Sometimes our prayers are purely selfish, and God doesn't answer that type either. As James wrote: "You ask and do not receive, because you asked wrongly, to spend it on your passions" (James 4:3, R.S.V.).

Sometimes the fault lies deeper. "If I regard iniquity in my heart," said David, "the Lord will not hear me" (Psalm 66:18). Unless we are truly sorry for our sins and genuinely want to be free from every evil thought, we can hardly expect a pure and holy God to help us.

"Behold, the Lord's hand is not shortened, that it cannot save; neither his ear heavy, that it cannot hear," wrote Isaiah: "but your iniquities have separated between you and your God, and your sins have hid his face from you, that he will not hear" (Isaiah 59:1, 2).

As much as God may wish to help us, cherished sin will keep Him from doing so. Like dirt in an electrical connection, sin stops the flow of power. Remove the dirt, give up the cherished sin, and the power will flow again.

We must be patient too. Just because a prayer isn't answered immediately, we must not assume that God will never answer it. "I waited patiently for the Lord," said David, "and he inclined unto me, and heard my cry" (Psalm 40:1). We must trust God to answer at the right time and in a way that will be best for us.

So keep on praying. Keep on talking to God. "Pray without ceasing" (1 Thessalonians 5:17). This doesn't mean that you must talk out loud to God all day long. It means living in a prayerful mood, thinking about God at every opportunity, being grateful to Him for all His goodness, quietly seeking His guidance and counsel about every problem. It means *habitually* "casting all your care upon him," knowing that "he careth for you" (1 Peter 5:7).

"Have no anxiety about anything," wrote the apostle Paul, "but in everything by prayer and . . . with thanksgiving let your requests be made known to God. And the peace of God, which passes all understanding, will keep your hearts and your minds in Christ Jesus" (Philippians 4:6, 7, R.S.V.).

Here indeed is more good news for you. By talking to God you can talk yourself out of trouble into peace, out of weakness into strength, out of anxiety into courage and new hope.

13

You Have a Friend
in Court

SOME TIME ago I received a bill from a collection agency in Los Angeles. At first glance I saw that it did not belong to me and promptly returned it.

Within a few days the bill came back, with a note attached urging prompt payment.

This time I wrote the firm a letter, requesting an explanation. Instead the bill came back a third time with a note reminding me that my credit rating was in peril.

So I wrote again, asking what it was all about. There was no answer, nothing but the same bill, this time with a veiled threat of legal proceedings.

In response to my fourth letter the bill came back with a curt statement that it had been referred to the firm's legal department for action.

By this time it dawned on me that I was in the grip of a soulless data-processing machine of some kind. Somehow my name had got into it and now it was spewing out documents of an increasingly threatening nature and there was nothing I could do about it.

That's when I thought about my attorney. I gave all the bills and letters to him and he took over. From his wide experience he knew exactly what to do. The bills stopped coming and I ceased to worry.

A friendly attorney can be of inestimable help in such a situation, or in any problem involving legal complications.

It is mighty comforting to have a friend in court, whether the court be on earth or in heaven.

Maybe you haven't needed the help of an attorney up to now, but one day you will, for the Bible says that God has "fixed a day on which he will judge the world" (Acts 17:31, R.S.V.).

Jesus was most explicit on this point, saying, "I tell you, on the day of judgment men will render account for every careless word they utter; for by your words you will be justified, and by your words you will be condemned" (Matthew 12:36, 37, R.S.V.).

This suggests that the coming judgment will have a comprehensiveness none of us has perhaps conceived. It pictures an investigation so thorough that every word and deed will be considered; and this in turn suggests the employment of an extremely elaborate system of recording.

Is such a system in operation? Has God arranged for a record to be kept of every word and deed of every person who has ever lived since the dawn of time?

It would seem so.

Note this passage from the book of Jeremiah. " ' "Ah Lord God!" ' " exclaimed the prophet. " ' "It is thou who hast made the heavens and the earth by thy great power and by thy outstretched arm! Nothing is too hard for thee, . . . O great and mighty God whose name is the Lord of hosts, great in counsel and mighty in deed; whose eyes are open to all the ways of men, rewarding every man according to his ways and according to the fruit of his doings" ' " (Jeremiah 32:17-19, R.S.V.).

The psalmist David had a similar conviction concerning God's total knowledge of every phase of his life, even of his thoughts. "O Lord," he said, "thou hast searched me and known me! Thou knowest when I sit down and when I rise up; thou discernest my thoughts from afar. Thou searchest out my path and my lying down, and art acquainted with all my ways. Even before a word is on my tongue, lo, O Lord, thou knowest it altogether. . . . Such knowledge is too wonderful for me; it is high, I cannot attain it.

11

"Whither shall I go from thy Spirit? Or whither shall I flee from thy presence? If I ascend to heaven, thou art there! If I make my bed in Sheol, thou art there! If I take the wings of the morning and dwell in the uttermost parts of the sea, even there thy hand shall lead me, and thy right hand shall hold me. If I say, 'Let only darkness cover me, and the light about me be night,' even the darkness is not dark to thee, the night is bright as the day; for darkness is as light with thee" (Psalm 139: 1-12, R.S.V.).

But God not only sees and hears everything that goes on; in some mysterious way He records it for use on the day of judgment when He will make the fateful decision as to who will share eternity with Him and who will not. This decision must be based on such clear and unquestionable evidence that all who look on—or who, millions of years hence, will look back upon it—will freely admit that His judgment is absolutely and perfectly just.

How and where are the records made? The Bible says that people will be judged by what is "written in the books" (Revelation 20:12). Daniel's description of the judgment also contains the statement that "the books were opened" (Daniel 7:10).

These "books" would not necessarily be like those

with which we are acquainted—made of paper, with leather bindings! They are much more likely to be highly complicated electronic devices, infinitely superior to any computer or data-processing machine man has so far invented. They could even be *living* computers, beings specially created for total observance and total recall. This is suggested in the fourth chapter of Revelation, where John tells how he saw four "living creatures" close to the throne of God "full of eyes in front and behind" and "full of eyes all round and within" (Revelation 4:6, 8, R.S.V.).

There is nothing unreasonable in this. Just think what man has already accomplished on his own initiative, in this matter of gathering and retaining information. Writing in the *Reader's Digest* for March, 1966, Brig. Gen. David Sarnoff said: "In the next five to ten years, high-power satellites hovering above the equator will broadcast television *directly* to set-owners anywhere in the world. . . . Long before the year 2000, man will be able to communicate instantaneously—in sound and sight, in written message and in exchanged computer information—with anyone anywhere. People in Stockholm, New York or Buenos Aires will be able to order, and receive almost at once, copies of business agreements, historical documents, photos and blueprints from anywhere else on this planet."—Page 66. (By permission of *Reader's Digest.*)

If such miracles are within man's grasp today, why limit the power and competence of the Creator and Sustainer of the universe?

Even though we may not know exactly how God is gathering and storing information about all who live upon the earth, we can be certain that He *is* doing it, and with the sole purpose of rendering judgment that shall be scrupulously just and fair.

This brings us face to face with a very vital matter. If God is gathering detailed information about everybody He is gathering it about us too. About you and me and our families, with all the sorry record we sometimes make.

But for one thing we could worry ourselves sick over a situation like this, wondering when God will come across our names in "the books" and what He will say about the tragic account of failure He finds there.

That one thing, however, makes all the difference. It is a provision He Himself has made for us.

John tells about it in his first letter: "If we walk in the light, as he is in the light, we have fellowship with one another, and the blood of Jesus his Son cleanses us from all sin. . . . If we confess our sins, he is faithful and

just, and will forgive our sins and cleanse us from all
unrighteousness. . . . But if any one does sin, *we have an
advocate with the Father, Jesus Christ the righteous"*
(1 John 1:7-2:1, R.S.V.).

Here is more good news. Great good news. We don't
need to worry about the judgment. An Advocate has
been provided for anyone who wants to avail himself of
His services. He will take anybody's case and care for it
—successfully.

"Jesus Christ the righteous" is willing to be our
Friend in court, our Attorney in the day of judgment.
We may roll all the burden of this problem upon Him
and He will look after everything for us.

All we have to do is to accept His gracious offer. As
we read in the Gospel of John, "God loved the world so
much that he gave his only Son, that everyone who has
faith in him may not die but have eternal life. It was not
to judge the world that God sent his Son into the world,
but that through him the world might be saved. The man
who puts his faith in him does not come under judgment; but the unbeliever has already been judged in that
he has not given his allegiance to God's only Son" (John
3:16-18, N.E.B.).

The same thought is conveyed in Revelation 3:5, 6,
where Jesus says concerning the person who is victorious

In the great judgment day, when we are judged by the
moral law given to Moses at Sinai, Christ will be the
advocate of every soul who trusts in Him.

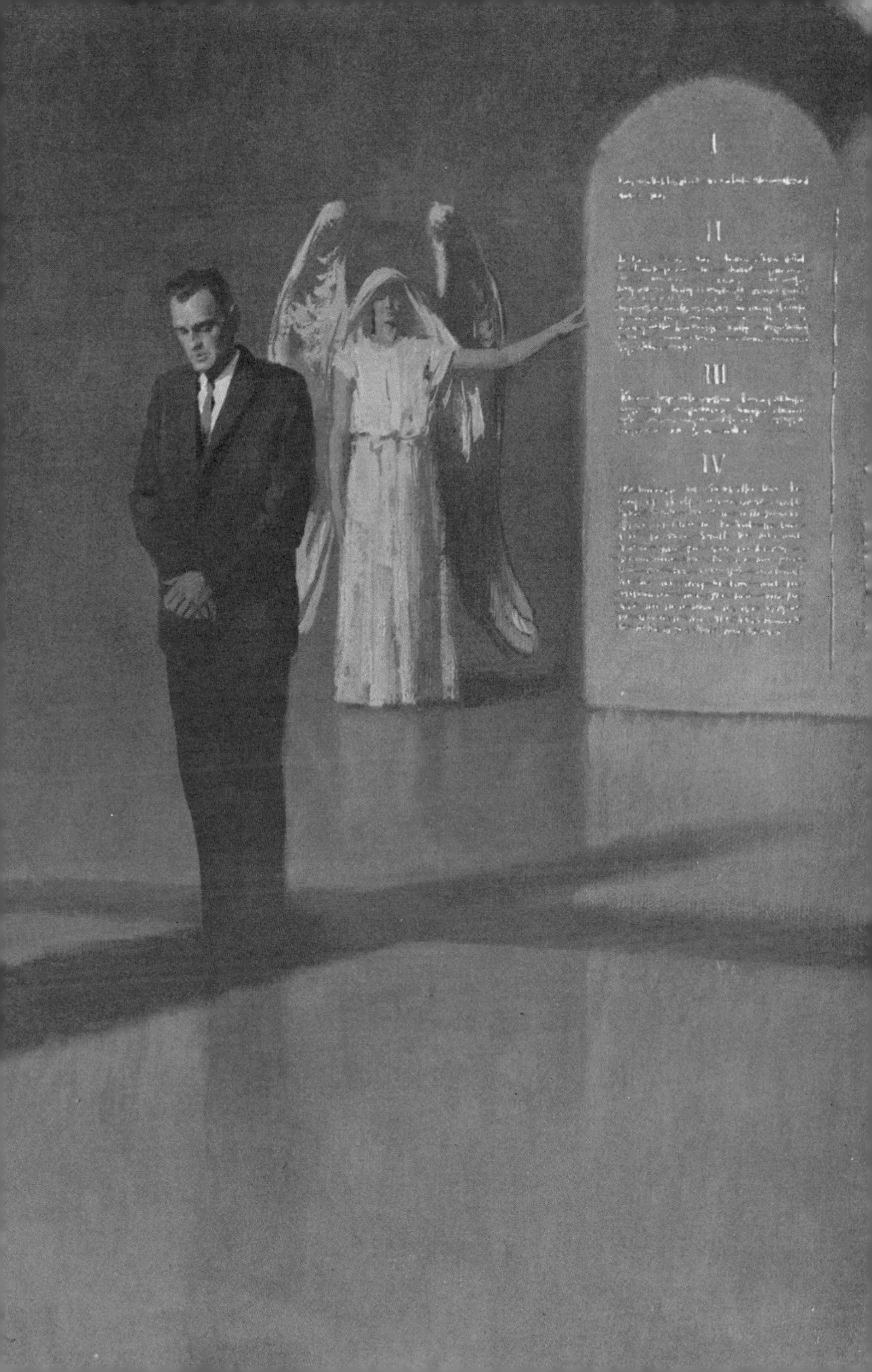
I
II
III
IV

over evil, " ' "his name I will never strike off the roll of the living, for in the presence of my Father and his angels *I will acknowledge him as mine*" ' " (N.E.B.).

That's what He will do for you in the judgment if here and now you stand with Him for righteousness and truth. Give Him your allegiance today, and He will claim you as His own tomorrow. When your name comes up for final decision He will say, "This is a friend of Mine. He loves Me. All his sins are forgiven. I want him to live with Me forever."

Because of His love for you, and all His gracious provisions on your behalf, you can "have confidence on the day of judgement" (1 John 4:17, N.E.B.).

That means you don't have to worry. You have a Friend in court. Your divine Attorney will care for everything.

In this "hour of his judgment" (Revelation 14:6, 7), be sure you put your case in His hands.

14

You Can Find God's People

TALKING TO GOD, studying the Bible, over-coming harmful habits, and generally living what is normally described as a good Christian life will bring blessings untold to you, to your family, and to others. It will make you a tower of strength in your community, a noble example to the rising generation.

It will do all this even if none of your immediate friends believe as you do—if you are standing alone, bucking a tide of godlessness, worldliness, and immorality. In such circumstances your faith may even grow stronger and your witness more potent as you meet opposition head on.

You will be encouraged, of course, as you meet others of like faith and similar purpose. Maybe you are looking for such people today—God's people, people who have cast their lot with God and are determined to be loyal

169

and true to Him in the midst of an evil and adulterous generation, people who accept the Bible as a message from God and seek to follow its teachings.

If you are looking for such people, I have more good news for you. You can find them.

Where are they? Everywhere.

In the first century A.D. the apostle Paul said that they —the "guileless" ones, those above reproach, "faultless children of God in a crooked and perverse generation"— *"shine like stars in a dark world"* (Philippians 2:14, 15, Moffatt).

I thought of this when visiting the famous Waitomo Caves in north New Zealand. Here, far underground, visitors are escorted by boat along a dark passage into a cave illuminated by the light of hundreds of thousands of glowworms. The ceiling looks for all the world like the sky on a clear star-lit night, presenting a striking symbolic picture of the people of God, glowing silently, faithfully, perennially, in a dark and evil world.

Many in all churches, Catholic and Protestant, are searching for such people today, eager to establish contact with them and unite with those holding the same principles and ideals.

I noticed this trend in Rome while attending the Vatican Council. That's when I first heard of the "crisis in

The Christ of the centuries, our contemporary Saviour, stretches forth His arms of invitation to all peoples.

obedience" in the church and learned that the chain of command, which has held this vast organization together for centuries, is breaking. "The three vows of the church used to be 'poverty, chastity and obedience,'" said one learned father, "but today they seem to be 'poverty, chastity and discussion.'" In other words, nobody wants to obey any more—neither youth, seminarians, nor priests. They all want to discuss first and obey afterward—if they feel like it.

The Declaration on Religious Freedom has encouraged the same trend, as has also the Declaration on Divine Revelation, which approves Biblical research by scholars and Bible study by the laity. As a result, many are making the shattering discovery that long-hallowed doctrines are not based on the Bible and have no link whatever with the faith of the early church. Hence their cautious looking around, wondering what to do and where to go.

Thousands of Protestants are in similar confusion, greatly troubled by the way their leaders have discarded the Bible as a book of myths and legends and rejected the concept of a personal God. They also are concerned at the seeming willingness of their leaders to sacrifice almost any doctrine that stands in the path of church unity.

In September of 1965 I attended the first meeting of the National Assembly of Evangelicals held in the Church House, Westminster, England. It had been called to discuss various aspects of the unity movement and its possible effect upon those who would not go along with it.

I shall never forget the speech of one Congregational minister. Addressing his fellow ministers, he said, "We have only a few months left. Within a year we will have to leave our churches, and where shall we go? We must set up a new organization of Bible-loving Christians so we shall have a spiritual home to go to."

It was a pitiful cry, and it made a deep impression on all who heard it. It brought into focus the vital fact that while church leaders are declaring the paramount need for unity, no matter what doctrinal beliefs must be surrendered in the process, many Bible-loving Christians are opposed to such a program. Rather than cause embarrassment, these good people are looking elsewhere for fellowship. Like this Congregational minister, they are asking, "Where shall we go?"

This is a most timely question and there should be an answer to it.

There is an answer.

God has prepared for this very situation. He has been

expecting it for a long time, for the Bible says, "The eyes of the Lord run to and fro throughout the whole earth, to shew himself strong in the behalf of them whose heart is perfect toward him" (2 Chronicles 16:9). The Berkeley Version renders this passage thus: "The eyes of the Lord flash back and forth over the whole earth to display His strength on behalf of those whose heart is full of integrity toward Him."

This has always been the case. God has ever been deeply concerned for those in every country whose lives are sincerely dedicated to Him, whose hearts are "full of integrity" toward Him. He is fully cognizant of all the honest in heart, all eager seekers after truth in every organization that has lost its way and is now in confusion. He sees them in "Babylon"—which is another name for confusion—and He calls to them in this hour of crisis, "Come out of her, my people" (Revelation 18:4).

Those who heed His call will find that He has indeed made ample provision for them to have fellowship with others who believe as they do; He has arranged that Bible-loving Christians of "every nation, and kindred, and tongue, and people" shall become members of one communion.

If you are looking for a spiritual home such as this, how will you recognize it? Naturally, you don't want to go from one unsatisfying state of affairs to another. You want certainty and you should have it.

You can have it. Such a fellowship will have certain distinctive characteristics that will stand out clear and sharp against the confusion of "Babylon." The delineation will be so striking that there will be no possibility of your making a mistake. You will know God's people when you find them, and they will be the very people you have been looking for.

Here are some of the outstanding marks to help you in your search.

1. *God's people will worship God.* This may seem elementary and superfluous. Not so today. Not when so many people are calling themselves "Christian atheists." Not when clergymen are boldly asserting that they cannot find evidence for God's existence anywhere. Not when the theory of evolution has seemingly driven God from His universe.

Bible-loving Christians will unite their voices in declaring their belief in a personal God, omnipotent and omniscient, Creator of the heavens and the earth. Their message to the world today will be "Fear God, and give glory to him; for the hour of his judgment is come: and worship him that made heaven, and earth, and the sea, and the fountains of waters" (Revelation 14:7).

Courageously they will hold fast to God's own declaration made on Sinai—"In six days the Lord made heaven and earth, the sea, and all that in them is" (Exodus 20:11).

If you find yourself in a group that denies God's existence or pokes fun at the Creation story, you will know you are in the wrong place.

2. *God's people will revere Jesus Christ as the Son of God.*

This too is fundamental and most urgent in a time when so many professed Christians deny the divinity of Christ and declare He was a good man but nothing more.

When Jesus asked His disciples, " 'Who do you say that I am?' Simon Peter replied, 'You are the Christ, the Son of the living God.' Jesus answered him, 'Blessed are you, Simon Bar-Jona! For flesh and blood has not revealed this to you, but my Father who is in heaven. And I tell you, you are Peter, and on this rock I will build my church, and the powers of death shall not prevail against it' " (Matthew 16:15-18, R.S.V.).

Not on Peter would He build His church, not on this rolling pebble soon to deny Him thrice, but on the great rock of truth that Peter had revealed—the divinity of Christ.

Nathanael had already discerned it, saying to Jesus, " 'You are the Son of God; you are king of Israel' " (John 1:49, N.E.B.).

The apostle Paul preached the same sublime truth —"God was in Christ, reconciling the world unto himself" (2 Corinthians 5:19).

Declared the apostle John: "Whoever confesses that Jesus is the Son of God, God abides in him, and he in God" (1 John 4:15, R.S.V.).

This is New Testament teaching. This is what the people of God believe. If you find yourself in a religious community that denies Christ's divinity, flee from it. You are in the wrong place.

3. *God's people will love the Bible.* They will regard it as *His* Book and therefore theirs. For while many words and phrases differ from one version to another, the great truths of the gospel revealed in all versions are without dispute the revelation of God's mind and will for the human race. Through this Book God spoke to men in ages past, and through it He speaks to modern man today.

In his second letter to Timothy, the apostle Paul wrote: "All scripture is inspired by God and profitable for teaching, for reproof, for correction, and for training in righteousness, that the man of God may be complete,

12

equipped for every good work" (2 Timothy 3:16, 17, R.S.V.).

Bidding farewell to the Christians in Ephesus, he said, "I commend you to God and to the word of his grace, which is able to build you up and to give you the inheritance among all those who are sanctified" (Acts 20:32, R.S.V.).

Likewise he wrote to the Romans: "For whatever was written in former days was written for our instruction, that by steadfastness and by the encouragement of the scriptures we might have hope" (Romans 15:4, R.S.V.).

Peter asserted that " 'the word of the Lord abides for ever,' " adding, "That word is the good news which was preached to you" (1 Peter 1:25, R.S.V.). He also wrote: "No prophecy ever came by the impulse of man, but men moved by the Holy Spirit spoke from God" (2 Peter 1:21, R.S.V.).

This is New Testament teaching. It reveals the attitude of the early Christians toward the Holy Scriptures. They revered them as the inspired Word of God. So will God's people today. They will be the people of a Book—God's Book.

Should you find yourself in a church where preachers and people scoff at the Bible and minimize its value, you may know you are in the wrong place.

4. *God's people will reveal the love of God in their lives.* Jesus Himself provided this mark. Said He: " 'By this all men will know that you are my disciples, if you have love for one another' " (John 13:35, R.S.V.).

In God's sight love is paramount. There is no substitute for it, nor can there be. Not the erection of buildings nor the giving of money. Not pompous titles or fancy degrees, gaudy vestments or elaborate ceremonies.

Paul understood this well. To the Corinthians he wrote these immortal words: "If I speak in the tongues of men and of angels, but have not love, I am a noisy gong or a clanging cymbal. And if I have prophetic powers, and understand all mysteries and all knowledge, and if I have all faith, so as to remove mountains, but have not love, I am nothing.

"If I give away all I have, and if I deliver my body to be burned, but have not love, I gain nothing.

"Love is patient and kind; love is not jealous or boastful; it is not arrogant or rude. Love does not insist on its own way; it is not irritable or resentful; it does not rejoice at wrong, but rejoices in the right. Love bears all things, believes all things, hopes all things, endures all things. . . . So faith, hope, love abide, these three; but the greatest of these is love" (1 Corinthians 13:1-13, R.S.V.).

The apostle John was most definite on this matter

also. "He who does not love does not know God," he said, "for God is love" (1 John 4:8, R.S.V.).

Again, "Beloved, let us love one another; for love is of God, and he who loves is born of God and knows God" (verse 7). And in verse 16: "God is love, and he who abides in love abides in God, and God abides in him."

This also is New Testament teaching. Now as then, God's people will be known by the love they manifest toward one another and toward those who don't belong to their group.

If you find yourself among people who are harsh and censorious, unkind and unforgiving, you will know they are not God's people and you will have to look elsewhere.

5. *God's people will hold the Ten Commandments in high regard.* This is narrowing the field quite a lot, for nowadays most Christians rarely give the Ten Commandments a single thought. They couldn't care less what they say.

Yet the Bible says: *"God* spake all these words." They are *His* words, God's words. And God's people will revere them and endeavor by divine grace to carry them out in their lives.

In case you have forgotten these commandments, here they are:

" 'You shall have no other gods before me.

" 'You shall not make yourself a graven image, or any likeness of anything that is in heaven above, or that is in the earth beneath, or that is in the water under the earth; you shall not bow down to them or serve them; for I the Lord your God am a jealous God, visiting the iniquity of the fathers upon the children to the third and the fourth generation of those who hate me, but showing steadfast love to thousands of those who love me and keep my commandments.

" 'You shall not take the name of the Lord your God in vain; for the Lord will not hold him guiltless who takes his name in vain.

" 'Remember the sabbath day, to keep it holy. Six days you shall labor, and do all your work; but the seventh day is a sabbath to the Lord your God; in it you shall not do any work, you, or your son, or your daughter, your manservant, or your maidservant, or your cattle, or the sojourner who is within your gates; for in six days the Lord made heaven and earth, the sea, and all that is in them, and rested the seventh day; therefore the Lord blessed the sabbath day and hallowed it.

" 'Honor your father and your mother, that your days may be long in the land which the Lord your God gives you.

" 'You shall not kill.

" 'You shall not commit adultery.

" 'You shall not steal.

" 'You shall not bear false witness against your neighbor.

" 'You shall not covet your neighbor's house; you shall not covet your neighbor's wife, or his manservant, or his maidservant, or his ox, or his ass, or anything that is your neighbor's' " (Exodus 20:3-17, R.S.V.).

These ten commandments constitute the moral law given by God for man's good. Enshrined in each commandment is a great moral principle which if followed will keep a man from harm and consequent unhappiness.

The first four commandments encourage love to God and the last six love to man. Jesus so summarized them when He said to an inquiring lawyer: " 'You shall love the Lord your God with all your heart, and with all your soul, and with all your mind. This is the great and first commandment. And a second is like it, You shall love your neighbor as yourself. On these two commandments depend all the law and the prophets' " (Matthew 22: 37-40, R.S.V.).

When asked if He had come to abolish the moral law He replied, " 'Think not that I have come to abolish the law and the prophets; I have come not to abolish them but to fulfil them. For truly, I say to you, till heaven and earth pass away, not an iota, not a dot, will pass from the law until all is accomplished' " (Matthew 5:17, 18, R.S.V.).

This also is New Testament teaching. Christ had the utmost respect for the Ten Commandments; and why not? Did He not give them to Moses in the first place?

So God's people today will respect His law. They will remember the Ten Commandments and try to live in harmony with them.

Should you find yourself among a group that speaks disrespectfully of the Ten Commandments and claims they were "done away" and made obsolete centuries ago, you will know you haven't yet found God's people, and will have to look somewhere else.

6. *God's people will observe God's Sabbath.* Surely this is reasonable. Why would they want to keep any other day? And which is God's day?

Read the fourth commandment again. It is as clear as God could make it. The King James Version says, "The seventh day is the sabbath of the Lord thy God." It couldn't be clearer. Certainly Jesus understood it perfectly, for it was His "custom" to attend the synagogue on this day (Luke 4:16, 31).

James A. Pike, for some years Episcopal bishop of San

Francisco, in his book *A Time for Christian Candor,* is candid on this point. Dealing with the fourth commandment he writes: "Since the earliest days of the Jewish-Christian community, most Christian churches have done nothing in particular about the Sabbath day unless a Holy Day happened to fall on a Saturday. The big event has been the celebration of the Holy Mysteries on the weekly feast of the Resurrection of Christ, namely, Sunday. The celebration of this day was not regarded as a substitute for the fulfilment of the Sabbath requirement in the Commandments (as is indicated by the fact that the first Jewish Christians also observed the Sabbath). . . . In the Anglican church this Commandment is read out solemnly once a month (when the rubric requiring it is observed), and the people respond, 'Lord, have mercy upon us, and incline our hearts to keep this law,' when, in fact, there is no intention whatsoever to keep this law (most of our churches having not so much as a service on that day)."—Page 40.

Just why Bishop Pike does not change his church procedure to harmonize with what he knows to be the truth he does not say, but at least his admission as to which day is the true Sabbath is helpful.

From this statement it is obvious that the Bible-loving Christian seeking God's people will be disappointed if he visits Grace Cathedral, or any other cathedral for that matter, on the seventh day, because he will find no services being held—no act of worship of any kind, nobody there at all. In order to worship on the Bible Sabbath, God's Sabbath, he will have to look elsewhere for his spiritual home.

7. *God's people will worship in simplicity.* Nowhere in the New Testament is there the slightest suggestion that the first Christians used elaborate ritual in their services. Most significant is the record that upon Christ's death on Calvary the veil of the Temple was "torn in two from top to bottom" (Matthew 27:51, N.E.B.), dramatically symbolizing the fact that the ancient services had served their purpose. Now that type had met antitype, further sacrifices would be meaningless, for we read in the book of Hebrews, "This man . . . offered one sacrifice for sins for ever" (chapter 10:12, K.J.V.). No more were needed or ever would be needed.

The celebration of the Lord's Supper was originally a very simple ceremony. In the early church it was like a family meal. This is how the apostle Paul described it: "I received from the Lord what I also delivered to you, that the Lord Jesus on the night when he was betrayed took bread, and when he had given thanks, he broke it, and said, 'This is my body which is for you. Do this in remembrance of me.' In the same way also the cup, after supper, saying, 'This cup is the new covenant in my blood. Do this, as often as you drink it, in remembrance of me.' For as often as you eat this bread and drink the cup, you proclaim the Lord's death until he comes" (1 Corinthians 11:23-26, R.S.V.).

No vestments, no elaborate ceremony, no frequent bowing, no endless repetition of set phrases. Only a simple, friendly service in memory of a Loved One departed but coming back again someday.

Inevitably, I thought of all this at the opening of Vatican II, when by the kindness of Catholic friends I sat for nearly four hours within a few feet of Pope Paul. The pomp and circumstance were awe-inspiring; the pageantry was magnificent; the blending of scarlet and gold a glorious "carrousel of color," to use Walt Disney's phrase. It was all thrilling beyond words. I wouldn't have missed it for anything. But it was as remote as the Pleiades from New Testament teaching. So far as I could see, there was nothing here that had the slightest link with apostolic Christianity.

Many Protestant churches today are introducing more and more ritual in an effort to recapture something they have lost and cannot recover. In this type of service the Bible-loving Christian does not feel at home. For the true simplicity of the gospel, he must look elsewhere.

8. *God's people will heed His counsels on health.* This also is reasonable, for surely those who belong to God will gladly follow His good advice, and as we noted in an earlier chapter, He has said much on the care and preservation of the body.

Through the apostle Paul the members of the church at Corinth were warned, "If any one destroys God's temple, God will destroy him. For God's temple is holy, and that temple you are" (1 Corinthians 3:16, 17, R.S.V.).

Because alcohol slowly but surely destroys the temple of God, His people will not touch it. They won't be occasional drinkers or moderate drinkers or problem drinkers or any other kind of drinker. They won't drink beer or wine or whisky or cocktails or anything that has alcohol in it. They won't drink it for their own sakes and for the sake of others, knowing that as God's people they should set an example of sobriety, particularly to the rising generation.

Because tobacco is known to be a principal cause of lung cancer and heart disease, and therefore a destroyer of the temple of God, His people will not smoke it in any form, whether in cigarettes, cigars, or pipes. They won't smoke it for their own good and for the good of others who may dislike and be harmed by its noxious fumes, and because, as God's people, they know they should set an example of self-control before the young.

Not long ago I stumbled by accident into a conference of ministers belonging to a certain Protestant denomination. Everyone present was smoking a huge cigar. The room was blue with smoke. I knew at once I was in the wrong place.

If you find yourself in a congregation where the members smoke and drink, you will know for sure that you are in the wrong place, that you haven't found God's people yet. You will have to keep on looking.

9. *God's people will cherish the Christian hope.* The hope that Christ will return someday is based on many wonderful promises and prophecies in God's Word. It has been the hope of God's people in every generation from the earliest times till now. As we shall see in a later chapter, patriarchs, prophets, and apostles bore united testimony to their confident belief that Christ will triumph at last over all evil and set up His kingdom of righteousness on the earth.

Jesus believed this Himself and made frequent reference to it. At the climax of His trial He said to the high priest: " 'Hereafter, you will see the Son of man seated at the right hand of Power and coming on the clouds of heaven' " (Matthew 26:64, R.S.V.).

The apostle Paul mentioned this hope many times in his writings, assuring Titus that "our blessed hope" is "the appearing of the glory of our great God and Savior Jesus Christ, who gave himself for us to redeem us from all iniquity and to purify for himself a people of his own who are zealous for good deeds" (Titus 2:13, 14, R.S.V.).

His use of the phrase "a people of his own" is significant. It is a clear reference to God's people. Evidently they will be a people who believe in and cherish the hope of Christ's return.

Hence if you should find yourself among people who make light of Christ's second advent you may know you are not among God's people. And if you belong to a church where you never hear a sermon on the subject from one year's end to the next, you have good reason to suspect that it is not God's church and you had better start looking for a new spiritual home.

10. *God's people will have His outlook on the world.* What is that? A mission field. God's people will see in every living person a soul for whom Christ died. Consequently they will have a mission program wide as the globe, embracing people of every race and color and country.

Ever in their minds will be their Lord's command: " 'Go forth to every part of the world, and proclaim the Good News to the whole creation'" (Mark 16:15, N.E.B.). Nor will they ever forget His thrilling prediction, " 'This gospel of the Kingdom will be proclaimed throughout the earth as a testimony to all nations; and then the end will come'" (Matthew 24:14, N.E.B.).

God's people will not confine their missionary activities to one locality, one country, or one continent. Like the angels of Revelation 14, they will fly with the "everlasting gospel" to "every nation, and kindred, and tongue, and people."

Their vision will be limitless, their compassion boundless. Their eyes will roam the earth for human need, and when they find it their hearts will follow, together with their money and service.

Should you find yourself in an organization that has little concern for promoting the cause of Christ in other lands, or in a church where offerings for overseas missions are so small that they reveal an almost total lack of interest in God's plan of redemption, you had better look elsewhere. You are in the wrong place.

There are still other identifying marks of God's people which may help you in your search. You will find that they follow the New Testament mode of baptism— by immersion. You will discover that they have a "diversity of gifts" such as Paul mentions in 1 Corinthians 12:

4-11—spiritual gifts for the help and blessing of the church. You will find that the members, by and large, are clean-living, law-abiding folks who pay their bills, honor their commitments, and share in all good causes. But don't expect perfection, for no one is perfect yet.

Maybe I have narrowed the field so much that you are beginning to get discouraged. I wouldn't be surprised if you are saying, "There are no people on earth like this. There couldn't be—not in a time like this."

If so, you are mistaken.

I have news for you. Good news. Such people *do* exist. They are here amid the world scene *now*—two million strong. And you can find them more easily than you think.

15

Your Chance
to Witness

WHILE IN Australia in 1964 I visited the Isle of the Dead, which is part of the old penal colony at Port Arthur, Tasmania. Here more than two thousand convicts and their guards were buried during the years that the settlement was in operation.

Wandering among the overgrown and long-forgotten tombstones, I chanced upon one bearing this inscription:

> "Robert Flowers, July 12, 1845
> "I left my nation and my home
> My country to defend.
> I here shall lay till the last day
> Till time shall have an end.
> When Jesus calls my dust shall rise
> When the last trumpet shall sound,
> With millions more ascend the skies
> By angels guarded round."

13   193

ecial days in the calendar year, like Thanksgiving,
ve opportunity to perform acts of charity to the
edy as expressions of Christian love.

As I read the quaint words it suddenly dawned upon me that under this tombstone lay the remains of one of God's people, a witness for Him in a dark and evil time. Among a gang of ruffians and unbelievers his faith in God held firm. To his grave he carried his love for Christ and his hope in the second advent of his Lord.

Another tomb—this one in an old English churchyard—bears the name of Dr. Peter Chamberlin (1601-1683). A lengthy inscription on it tells how he was court physician to three Stuart kings of England—James I, Charles I, and Charles II—and their queens, also that "he was a Christian keeping the commandments of God and the faith of Jesus, being baptized about the year 1648 and keeping the seventh day for the Sabbath above 32 years."

At a time of great national upheaval, including Cromwell's rebellion and the restoration of the monarchy, when the morals of the court were notoriously bad, this noble doctor remained loyal to God and His commandments.

Similar tombstones dot the earth, ofttimes in out-of-the-way places rarely seen by the milling crowds of the twentieth century. Moss-grown and crumbling in decay, they tell the thrilling truth that in every century, as far back as history goes, God has had His faithful witnesses who have loved, honored, and served Him, ofttimes against great odds, and carried to their graves the hope of Christ's return in glory.

In the course of his missionary journeys the apostle Paul told the wildly excited throng at Lystra that "in times past" God "left not himself without witness" (Acts 14: 16, 17). How right he was! From the dawn of history, even in the darkest times, there have been those who have stood bravely for righteousness and truth.

The *New English Bible* renders this passage: " 'He has not left you without some clue to his nature' "—a most precious thought. Always, in one way or another, God has left a clue to His nature, the most convincing being the noble, dedicated lives of His people—people who revere His name, believe His Word, keep His commandments, observe His Sabbath, and by their blameless lives proclaim their loyalty to Him. What a " 'clue to his nature' " are such as these!

Even as God has had His witnesses in times past, so He has them today. There is something special about them, too, for they have appeared on the world scene at this time in answer to a remarkable prophecy in the book of Revelation.

The fourteenth chapter contains the thrilling prediction of a mighty religious revival in the years immediately preceding Christ's return. It tells of a message from heaven being carried swiftly—on the wings of angels— to the entire population of the globe. This message warns of the dire consequences of denying God and rebelling against Him; it calls the honest in heart to come out of the confusion of Babylon and take their stand boldly for Him; and it bids all men "Fear God, and give glory to him; for the hour of his judgment is come" (verse 7).

Then follows this description of those who heed this message: "Here are they that keep the commandments of God, and the faith of Jesus" (verse 12).

In other words, here are God's people of the last days, His witnesses amid all the troubles, all the wickedness, all the religious confusion of the twentieth century.

In Elijah's day, when it seemed as though the entire nation of Israel had turned from the worship of God to the idolatry of Baal, the prophet said, "I, even I only, am left." He thought he was the last of the loyalists. Not so, said God. You are mistaken. "I have left me seven thousand in Israel, all the knees which have not bowed unto Baal" (1 Kings 19:18).

So today, when it sometimes appears that Christianity is fading out, its faith destroyed by science or suffocated by modernism and the new atheism, a voice from above cries, "Be of good cheer! I have thousands left who still believe in Me. Look around you. Behold them in every nation and denomination. Here they are. Here, and here, and here! See how they keep God's commands and remain loyal to Jesus."

How and when did this loyalist movement begin?

It grew out of the great religious revival of the 1840's. At that time there was more Bible study than there had been for decades. Bible prophecies were examined with unprecedented care. Gradually the conviction spread that the time of the end had arrived, that God was about to close His account with the nations, and that one last effort must be made to carry the gospel to mankind.

People belonging to diverse organizations met, and finding mutual agreement, coalesced to form what was to become in later years the great Second Advent Movement, with mission outposts around the globe.

The beginnings were small. In fact, the original group was composed of only a handful of young people. But their faith and courage were prodigious and their vision limitless. Of financial resources they had none, but this did not trouble them. No sacrifice was too great to aid the cause they had espoused. Every talent they possessed was used to the full.

As others joined the movement and their talents were employed, all caught the same zealous spirit, and like the early disciples they went everywhere "preaching the word" (Acts 11:19).

For the first thirty years their efforts were confined to the United States, but as their numbers and resources grew they lifted their sights, and in 1874 sent their first missionary overseas. He planted the banner of the Advent Movement in Basel, Switzerland, from which center its message spread through all Europe. Bible-loving Christians in many countries decided that this was what they had been waiting for. They loved the simplicity of the movement, its loyalty to "the commandments of God and the faith of Jesus," and its adherence to New Testament teachings and practices.

Some came out of the Catholic Church, some from the Greek Orthodox Church, others from the Church of England, and still others from old religious organizations in Germany, Holland, Norway, Sweden, Denmark, Turkey, Armenia, and Russia. As they joined the movement they brought their talents, each one eager to spread the good news as best he could. Thus, despite severe opposition in many places their work grew and prospered.

Meanwhile, in 1885, a small group of pioneers sailed from San Francisco for Australia to proclaim the Advent message there. Starting in Melbourne, they moved on to Sydney, Adelaide, Perth, and dozens of smaller towns and villages. Some of them crossed the Tasman Sea to New Zealand and began to labor in Auckland, Napier, Hastings, Christchurch, and Dunedin. Everywhere they found seekers after truth who rejoiced to learn of the existence of a people espousing such high moral principles and such total loyalty to God and the Bible. As these joined the growing church they also brought *their* talents, and the work grew and multiplied, spreading through all the islands of the South Pacific. Today more than seventy thousand commandment keepers live in that area.

In 1890 four families rejoicing in the Advent hope arrived in Argentina from the United States, becoming for several weeks the only representatives of the Advent Movement in all South America. Faithfully they bore witness to the truths they believed. Others joined them. Four years later a preacher arrived from the United States and a church was organized. Decade after decade the message swept on across prairies, through jungles, and up into the high Andes. Today, in all the countries of this great continent 342,000 communicants stand loyally for "the commandments of God and the faith of Jesus."

Thus has it happened in all the continents of earth. First a lone pioneer arrived, Bible in hand, with little but his own courage to sustain him. Within a year or two, dozens of truth seekers joined him. These in turn, pooling their talents, broadened the area of witness until the remotest places were reached. By the end of 1966 the total membership in all the world was nearly two million.

All these have not come out of Catholic or Protestant churches. Many have come from Hinduism, Mohammedanism, Confucianism, and the devil-worshiping religions of Africa and elsewhere. This movement actually numbers within its ranks many a former cannibal and headhunter, and hundreds of the stone-age tribesmen of New Guinea. It has found that the gospel of Christ is indeed the power of God unto salvation, working miracles of character transformation.

Besides preaching the Word and uplifting Christ as Saviour and coming King, these people have ministered to the sick on a global scale, believing that this is what the Lord would have them do. At immense cost they have built a chain of 128 hospitals and sanitariums around the world, plus 165 clinics and dispensaries, manning them with 18,000 employees, including some 500 physicians and surgeons.

To speed the proclamation of their message they have established 44 publishing houses, employing more than 2,000 workers, and printing books, periodicals, and tracts in 228 languages.

To provide their youth with a Christian education they operate two universities, 431 colleges and secondary schools and nearly 5,000 elementary schools.

To help the poor and needy they have set up a worldwide chain of welfare and disaster-relief agencies that handle vast supplies of food and clothing, particularly in times of emergency.

To support all this global activity they contribute liberal sums of money and are none the poorer for doing so. Their tithes and offerings for 1964 amounted to more than $127,630,000.

But it isn't the money or the institutions or the prestige they now enjoy that marks these people as God's people. It is what they believe and teach—the basic principles for which they stand.

In a time when atheism flourishes, they believe in God, the Creator and Sustainer of the universe.

In an hour when Christ is being demoted to a mere man, they hold that He is the divine Son of God.

While many are discarding the Bible as obsolete, they declare it to be God's Book for modern man.

In an age of lawlessness, crime, and corruption, they point to the Ten Commandments as the abiding moral law, God's standard of right doing for the human race.

While the world rushes madly on in its seven-day-a-week program of work and pleasure, they faithfully dedicate each seventh day to worshiping God.

In addition they practice Bible baptism, celebrate the Lord's Supper in New Testament simplicity, return a tithe of their increase to God, and in every way try to live in a manner well-pleasing to Him.

Most likely some of these people live in your town, maybe on your street. If you would like to meet them, just mention "the commandments of God and the faith of Jesus" and the glow in their eyes will give them away.

Someday you may want to join them. Think about it. Pray about it. Maybe this is just what you should do.

And here is more good news for you. If you have dreamed of making your life truly meaningful, of casting your influence always on the side of that which is right and true, of using your talents to the limit in the service of God and your fellow man, your dream can come true now! This is your chance to witness for God, to do something splendid for Him.

Many and great will be the blessings it will bring you.

16

Christ on His Way

FAMILIAR AS Christmas is the story of the angel and the Bethlehem shepherds, and how he said to them: " 'I have good news for you: there is great joy coming to the whole people. . . . You will find a baby lying all wrapped up, in a manger' " (Luke 2:10-13, N.E.B.). Less well known is the record of the angelic visit to the other shepherds—the shepherds of Olivet—appointed such by the Chief Shepherd to feed His sheep and His lambs.

On this occasion the angels said, " 'Men of Galilee, why stand there looking up into the sky? This Jesus, who has been taken away from you up to heaven, will come in the same way as you have seen him go' " (Acts 1:11, N.E.B.).

Thus it was that both at His coming and at His departing the angels brought good news—first of His arrival in a

203

stable, second of His coming in glory. Both were designed to bring great joy to all the people.

The post-ascension meeting was not, of course, the first time the disciples had heard about their Lord's return. He Himself had told them of it on several occasions.

In words they would never forget, He had said to them: " 'Set your troubled hearts at rest. Trust in God always; trust also in me. There are many dwelling-places in my Father's house; if it were not so I should have told you; for I am going there on purpose to prepare a place for you. And if I go and prepare a place for you, I shall come again and receive you to myself, so that where I am you may be also' " (John 14:1-3, N.E.B.).

In answer to their question as to *when* He would come, He had assured them that He would give due warning of His return with an abundance of signs in heaven and earth, so none need be caught unawares. After that He had said they would "see the Son of man coming in the clouds of heaven with power and great glory" (Matthew 24:30).

On another occasion He had pictured to them His day of triumph when "the Son of man shall come in his glory, and all the holy angels with him" and He shall "sit upon the throne of his glory" (Matthew 25:31).

So the disciples were well aware of His promise to re-

t the ascension of Christ, angels told the disciples, This Jesus, who has been taken away from you . . . rill come again . . . as you have seen him go."

turn as they stood there watching His solemn departure, but their faith may well have been strained to the limit when at last He disappeared from view. And then it was that the angels came with His personal assurance that He would never forget them and that He would surely return someday.

As they descended the mountain and made their way to Jerusalem and the upper room, their hearts were overflowing with confidence and holy joy. Not only had they watched their beloved Lord vanish into the skies, they had heard from angel lips His promise to come again.

No wonder that in their proclamation of the gospel message they linked His resurrection with His second coming. Christ risen from the dead; Christ coming again as King of kings and Lord of lords: such was the good news they carried to the people of their day. No wonder it swept like a prairie fire through the Roman Empire and turned the whole world upside down!

These twin truths appear again and again in the New Testament Epistles.

To the Corinthians, Paul wrote: "For as by a man came death, by a man has come also the resurrection of the dead. For as in Adam all die, so also in Christ shall all be made alive. But each in his own order: Christ the first fruits, then at his coming those who belong to Christ.

Then comes the end, when he delivers the kingdom to God the Father after destroying every rule and every authority and power. For he must reign until he has put all his enemies under his feet" (1 Corinthians 15: 21-25, R.S.V.).

In the same chapter he told of the tremendous events that will occur at Christ's return when "we shall all be changed, in a moment, in the twinkling of an eye, at the last trumpet. For the trumpet will sound, and the dead will be raised imperishable, and we shall be changed. For this perishable nature must put on the imperishable, and this mortal nature must put on immortality" (verses 51-53, R.S.V.).

To the church at Thessalonica he sent these encouraging words: "Since we believe that Jesus died and rose again, even so, through Jesus, God will bring with him those who have fallen asleep. For this we declare to you by the word of the Lord, that we who are alive, who are left until the coming of the Lord, shall not precede those who have fallen asleep. For the Lord himself will descend from heaven with a cry of command, with the archangel's call, and with the sound of the trumpet of God. And the dead in Christ will rise" (1 Thessalonians 4:14-16, R.S.V.).

Notice how in both these letters the apostle linked

the resurrection of Christ with His return in glory. The two great doctrines are inseparable. One complements the other. As Paul also said, "If there is no resurrection of the dead, then Christ has not been raised; if Christ has not been raised, then our preaching is in vain. . . . We are even found to be misrepresenting God" (1 Corinthians 15:13-15, R.S.V.).

The Epistle to the Hebrews contains the same dynamic message. In the ninth chapter we read: "So Christ, having been offered once to bear the sins of many, will appear a second time, not to deal with sin but to save those who are eagerly waiting for him" (verse 28, R.S.V.).

In the following chapter the reader is exhorted: "Do not throw away your confidence, which has a great reward. . . . 'For yet a little while, and the coming one shall come and shall not tarry' " (verses 35-37, R.S.V.).

Likewise the Gospel of John and the book of Revelation, written long after Paul had gone to his rest, and decades after Christ's ascension, are full of references to these two basic teachings of the Christian faith.

In the first chapter of Revelation John reports having met the living Christ, who said to him: " 'Fear not, I am the first and the last, and the living one; I died, and behold I am alive for evermore' " (verses 17, 18, R.S.V.).

Then in the nineteenth chapter he records this sub-lime vision of Christ's second coming: "I saw heaven opened, and behold, a white horse! He who sat upon it is called Faithful and True, and in righteousness he judges and makes war. His eyes are like a flame of fire, and on his head are many diadems. . . . He is clad in a robe dipped in blood, and the name by which he is called is The Word of God. And the armies of heaven, arrayed in fine linen, white and pure, followed him. . . . On his robe and on his thigh he has a name inscribed, King of kings and Lord of lords" (verses 11-16, R.S.V.).

The language is symbolic, but its intent is clear. The resurrected One, the living Christ, will one day return—not as a Babe in a stable but as Ruler of the nations and Judge of all mankind.

With such solid New Testament backing for these great truths it was but natural that they would find their way into the creeds of Christendom. For instance, the Apostles' Creed, which dates back, in substance, to the third century A.D., begins like this:

"I believe in God the Father Almighty, Maker of heaven and earth: And in Jesus Christ his only Son our Lord: Who was conceived by the Holy Ghost, Born of the Virgin Mary: Suffered under Pontius Pilate, Was crucified, dead, and buried: He descended into hell; The

14

third day he rose again from the dead: He ascended into heaven, And sitteth on the right hand of God the Father Almighty: From thence he shall come to judge the quick and the dead."—*The Book of Common Prayer*, p. 284.

This creed has been recited by Christians of various communions for at least sixteen centuries. Even today it is used almost every Sunday in Anglican and Episcopalian churches round the world, serving to keep these fundamental truths in mind even though, in all too many places, it has become a hollow ritual, a recitation of words without meaning.

Strangely, it is the great Second Advent Movement that is giving new life to this dead or dying formula. Its members may not use the ancient creed as such, but they agree with every word of it. It states basic Bible truth, and that's what they believe. It is a definite link with the early church, and they want to be linked with that church.

That's why they say they are giving the "everlasting gospel" to the world. They are indeed—the same gospel the early church preached, adapted to the twentieth century; the good news of a risen Christ who is coming back to the earth again, with added emphasis on the imminence of His return.

Hebrews 10:12, 13 reads: "This man, after he had offered one sacrifice for sins for ever, sat down on the right hand of God; *from henceforth expecting* till his enemies be made his footstool."

"This man" has been "expecting" for more than nineteen hundred years. Now the waiting time is almost over. Hence the warning message now being carried everywhere by God's people: "Fear God, and give glory to him; for the hour of his judgment is come" (Revelation 14:7).

"This same Jesus" is about to return—the One who loved the poor, the sick, the needy; the One who showed kindness to sinners, sympathy to mourners, gentleness to children; the One who was always thinking of others, never of Himself; the One who stood for right, insisted upon truth, exposed hypocrites, defied tyrants, challenged the hierarchy; the One who calmed the sea, cast out devils, raised the dead; the kindest, most gracious, most understanding Person who ever lived. He is coming back to this earth, crowned with glory and honor; coming to set up His kingdom of righteousness, peace, and love; coming to reign for all eternity.

He is on His way. What good news is this!

In the words of Caroline Noel's beautiful poem,

> "At the name of Jesus
> Every knee shall bow,
> Every tongue confess Him
> King of glory now;

'Tis the Father's pleasure
    We should call Him Lord,
Who from the beginning
    Was the mighty Word.

"In your hearts enthrone Him;
    There let Him subdue
All that is not holy,
    All that is not true;
Crown Him as your Captain
    In temptation's hour;
Let His will enfold you
    In its light and power.

"Brothers, this Lord Jesus
    Shall return again,
With His Father's glory,
    With His angel train;
For all wreaths of empire
    Meet upon His brow,
And our hearts confess Him
    King of glory now."

—*Old Favorite Songs and Hymns*—
Richard Charlton MacKenzie, ed.
(c. 1946), Garden City Pub. Co.

17

No Need to Doubt

HOW CERTAIN can we be that Christ will come again? Is this hope real or a figment of the imagination? Is it truly good news?

Strangely, the promise of Christ's return is the only one in all the Bible to which the words "certain" and "sure" are attached. They occur at the close of one of the most remarkable prophecies in all the Scriptures—one so accurate in its delineation of the future that it makes the predictions of certain modern prophets and prophetesses cheap and foolish by comparison.

"The dream is certain, and the interpretation thereof sure," declared the prophet Daniel.

He was referring to the dream of Nebuchadnezzar, king of Babylon, and to the interpretation which, by divine inspiration, he had just given it. Because this dream and interpretation have a direct bearing on Christ's sec-

213

ond advent, and therefore have enormous significance to everyone alive today, I retell the story here.

While still a young man Nebuchadnezzar had a dream one night that made a great impression on his mind. By morning, however, he had forgotten it. All that remained was a deep conviction that it had some profound and urgent meaning.

The more he tried to recall the dream, the more frustrated he became. At last he decided to seek help from his counselors, including magicians, astrologers, sorcerers, and other dealers in the occult.

"Tell us the dream," they said, "and we will interpret it for you."

"That's the trouble," said the king, in effect. "I can't. The thing is gone from me."

Now the counselors were in trouble. They could concoct an interpretation without difficulty, but to describe the dream itself was something else again. It would be too easy to guess wrong.

"Nobody can do this," they said.

The king coaxed. He offered bribes. But to no effect. The counselors were helpless.

Losing patience, he began to threaten. If they did not tell him his dream, he would have them cut in pieces and their houses destroyed. Still they were silent.

The great image of Daniel 2 that Nebuchadnezzar saw in his dream portrayed the successive empires of earth that would flourish until Jesus comes.

At last, becoming "very furious," he called the captain of the guard and gave orders that all the wise men of Babylon should be slain.

At this point Daniel entered the picture. Though still but a youth, because of his proved sagacity his name had already been added to the list of the city's wise men. Consequently, the guard turned up at his door to arrest him.

Shocked by the drastic nature of the order, Daniel pleaded for time, promising the king that he would be told his dream.

Now he had to deliver, and fast. Calling three of his Hebrew friends together, he sought God earnestly for help. That night he was shown both the king's dream and its interpretation.

"Blessed be the name of God for ever and ever," he cried out in heartfelt gratitude, "for wisdom and might are his: and he changeth the times and the seasons: he removeth kings, and setteth up kings: he giveth wisdom unto the wise, and knowledge to them that know understanding: he revealeth the deep and secret things: he knoweth what is in the darkness, and the light dwelleth with him. I thank thee, and praise thee, O thou God of my fathers, who hast given me wisdom and might, and hast made known unto me now what we desired of thee:

for thou hast now made known unto us the king's matter" (Daniel 2:20-23).

Ushered into the presence of Nebuchadnezzar, the young captive stood before him without fear. Having talked with the King of kings, why should he quail before the ruler of an earthly empire? Nor did he question for one moment that the dream he was about to recite was correct in every detail.

"Can you tell me my dream?" asked Nebuchadnezzar.

"I can't," said Daniel humbly, "but God can. There is a God in heaven who reveals secrets, and makes known what shall be in the latter days."

He then recounted the dream.

"Thou, O king, sawest, and behold a great image," he said, as the king leaned forward with ever-increasing fascination. "This great image, whose brightness was excellent, stood before thee; and the form thereof was terrible.

"This image's head was of fine gold, his breast and his arms of silver, his belly and his thighs of brass, his legs of iron, his feet part of iron and part of clay.

"Thou sawest till that a stone was cut out without hands, which smote the image upon his feet that were of iron and clay, and brake them to pieces.

"Then was the iron, the clay, the brass, the silver, and the gold, broken to pieces together, and became like the chaff of the summer threshingfloors; and the wind carried them away, that no place was found for them: and the stone that smote the image became a great mountain, and filled the whole earth" (verses 31-35).

The light in the king's eyes and the glow upon his face must have been something to see. For Daniel had described exactly what he had beheld in his dream, in all its gripping reality.

Silent in wonder, he waited for this extraordinary youth to proceed.

"This is the dream," continued Daniel; "and we will tell the interpretation thereof before the king" (verse 36).

Humbly, sincerely, confidently, he proceeded to impart the most startling revelation ever made to any monarch:

"Thou, O king, art a king of kings: for the God of heaven hath given thee a kingdom, power, and strength, and glory. And wheresoever the children of men dwell, the beasts of the field and the fowls of the heaven hath he given into thine hand, and hath made thee ruler over them all. Thou art this head of gold.

"And after thee shall arise another kingdom inferior

to thee, and another third kingdom of brass, which shall bear rule over all the earth.

"And the fourth kingdom shall be strong as iron: forasmuch as iron breaketh in pieces and subdueth all things: and as iron that breaketh all these, shall it break in pieces and bruise.

"And whereas thou sawest the feet and toes, part of potters' clay, and part of iron, the kingdom shall be divided; but there shall be in it of the strength of the iron, forasmuch as thou sawest the iron mixed with miry clay.

"And as the toes of the feet were part of iron, and part of clay, so the kingdom shall be partly strong, and partly broken.

"And whereas thou sawest iron mixed with miry clay, they shall mingle themselves with the seed of men: but they shall not cleave one to another, even as iron is not mixed with clay.

"And in the days of these kings shall the God of heaven set up a kingdom, which shall never be destroyed: and the kingdom shall not be left to other people, but it shall break in pieces and consume all these kingdoms, and it shall stand for ever.

"Forasmuch as thou sawest that the stone was cut out of the mountain without hands, and that it brake in pieces the iron, the brass, the clay, the silver, and the gold; the great God hath made known to the king what shall come to pass hereafter: and *the dream is certain, and the interpretation thereof sure*" (verses 37-45).

Suddenly these two young men found themselves gazing upon a panorama never before seen by human eyes. For this was no mere recital of a dream; it was a revelation of all history to be.

As the veil of the future was mysteriously withdrawn, they looked out together across the vast expanse of unborn centuries. They saw the rise and fall of kingdoms yet unknown. They saw mysterious conquerors come and go. They beheld the strife and turmoil of rival nations in our time. And they gazed at last upon the King of kings coming in power and glory to set up a kingdom that shall endure forever.

Sublime, magnificent vista!

No wonder Nebuchadnezzar exclaimed in mingled amazement and humility: "Of a truth it is, that your God is a God of gods, and a Lord of kings, and a revealer of secrets" (verse 47).

That was about 603 B.C. Twenty-five centuries have passed since then—centuries that could so easily have proved Daniel's interpretation both false and foolish. They have not. Instead, every detail has come to pass; everything, that is, except the final climactic event.

Four world empires have come upon the stage of history exactly as predicted.

When Babylon's day was done the scepter passed to Medo-Persia, inferior in wealth and majesty as silver is to gold but greater far in strength. Then followed Greece, the mighty kingdom of brass, led by Alexander the Great.

Disintegrating in time, Greece gave place to Rome, the fourth kingdom which, strong as iron, broke in pieces and completely subdued the whole Mediterranean world.

In course of time Rome, too, came to its end. Weakened by internal corruption, hard-pressed by barbarian tribes, it fell into ten divisions—namely, the Anglo-Saxons, the Franks, the Alamanni, the Lombards, the Ostrogoths, the Visigoths, the Burgundians, the Vandals, the Suevi, and the Heruli. Seven of these may be clearly traced to the nations of modern Europe.

For nearly fifteen hundred years these fragments of iron and clay have been in existence, with one strong man after another striving in vain to unite them once more into one great whole. Time and again the attempt has been made—by Charlemagne, by Charles V, by Louis XIV, by Napoleon, by Kaiser Wilhelm, by Adolf Hitler —but every one has failed. Some tried treaties; some tried intermarriage; some tried war; but all came to the same frustrating end. Blocking every attempt at reunion were the seven fateful words of the divine edict, "They shall not cleave one to another."

These are the words that defeated Hitler and all the great conquerors who preceded him. They are the words that will bring to ruin every aspirant to European or world dominion who may arise in the future.

No matter what apparent unity may be achieved, either by political or commercial agreements such as the Common Market and other devices, the Continent will remain divided at heart, ready to separate at any moment of stress. There will always be someone in one country or another to break up the party.

But now look again at the climax of the prediction: "In the days of these kings shall the God of heaven set up a kingdom, which shall never be destroyed: and the kingdom shall not be left to other people, but it shall break in pieces and consume all these kingdoms, and it shall stand for ever" (verse 44).

This is nothing less than a description of the tremendous, earth-shaking scenes to take place when Christ shall return in glory and power.

When will they occur?

"In the days of these kings," or kingdoms; in the days when the ancient Roman Empire is still divided; in the days of the diverse and ever-bickering governments of modern Europe. *In these days* God will intervene to bring all earthly kingdoms to an end.

Note well that the stone "cut out without hands" smites the image *"upon his feet,"* at the very bottom of it, in the last days of history. It will break both feet and toes in pieces, then fill the whole earth with the glory of the Lord (verses 34, 35).

There is no time setting here, no hint that Christ will come in some precise year or decade. Nevertheless, there is the clearest evidence of the *period* in which He will reappear. That period has arrived.

As certainly as Medo-Persia followed Babylon in the sequence of empires, as certainly as Greece took over Medo-Persia's dominion, as certainly as Rome seized the scepter from Greece, as certainly as Rome remains divided to this day, so certainly will Christ return while these divisions remain.

No matter how many people claim that His second coming is unthinkable in the space age, no matter that Bishop James Pike and others like him declare that Christ was mistaken in His eschatology, no matter what *anyone* says to the contrary, this great prophecy in the second chapter of Daniel stands as a mighty bulwark of the "blessed hope," which cannot and will not be overthrown.

"The dream is certain, and the interpretation thereof sure."

18

Not Long to Wait

WHILE WE may be certain of the *period* of history in which Christ will return—"the days of these kings"—the actual date of His second coming has not been revealed, and for very good reason. Were it known, most people would neglect preparation for it until too late.

God knows the day and the hour, of course, but nobody else knows. He has kept this vital information strictly to Himself, not even telling the angels, lest somehow they should pass it on and the "powers of darkness" get hold of it. Christ did not bring it with Him when He came to sojourn among men for a few brief years. Said He: " 'About that day and hour, no one knows, not even the angels in heaven, not even the Son; only the Father' " (Matthew 24:36, N.E.B.).

Even after His resurrection, when His disciples asked

15

← PAINTING BY WILLIAM HUTCHINSON   © 1956 BY REVIEW AND HERALD

The most glorious imminent event in the history of the world will be the personal, visible coming of Christ to earth as Lord of lords and King of kings.

Him pointedly, " 'Lord, is this the time when you are to establish once again the sovereignty of Israel?' he answered, 'It is not for you to know about dates or times, which the Father has set within his own control' " (Acts 1:6, 7, N.E.B.).

While time setting is "out," watching for promised signs is definitely "in." Christ was most explicit on this point. He wants His people to be ever alert for evidence of the imminence of His return.

" 'Watch therefore,' " He said to His disciples, " 'for you do not know on what day your Lord is coming' " (Matthew 24:42, R.S.V.).

Again: " 'Take heed to yourselves lest your hearts be weighed down with dissipation and drunkenness and cares of this life, and that day come upon you suddenly like a snare. . . . But watch at all times, praying that you may have strength to escape all these things that will take place, and to stand before the Son of man' " (Luke 21:34-36, R.S.V.).

To illustrate His point He called attention to a nearby tree, saying, " 'Look at the fig tree, and all the trees; as soon as they come out in leaf, you see for yourselves and know that the summer is already near. So also, when you see these things taking place, you know that the kingdom of God is near' " (verses 29-31).

It is as simple as that. Watching for His coming is like watching leaves appear in the spring—seeing brown, dead branches turn swiftly to vivid green.

What signs did Jesus say would appear? What did He have in mind when He spoke of "these things"?

There would be *signs in the heavens,* He said, in " 'sun and moon and stars' " (Luke 21:25, R.S.V.). " 'Terrors and great signs from heaven' " (verse 11). More specifically, " 'the sun will be darkened, and the moon will not give its light, and the stars will fall from heaven, and the powers of the heavens will be shaken' " (Matthew 24:29, R.S.V.).

There would also be *signs in the earth,* including " 'great earthquakes, and in various places famines and pestilences' " (Luke 21:11, R.S.V.).

In addition there would be *signs among the nations* for " 'nation will rise against nation, and kingdom against kingdom' " (verse 10, R.S.V.). As a result there would be " 'upon the earth distress of nations, . . . men fainting with fear and with foreboding of what is coming on the world' " (verses 25, 26, R.S.V.). The *New English Bible* renders this passage thus: " 'On earth nations will stand helpless, not knowing which way to turn from the roar and surge of the sea; men will faint with terror at the thought of all that is coming upon the world.' "

Not universal peace but global trouble was the picture He painted.

There would also be *signs in social affairs,* particularly a plunge into moral anarchy akin to that which preceded the flood of Noah's day. Said Jesus, " 'As it was in the days of Noah, so shall it be in the days of the Son of man. They ate, they drank, they married, they were given in marriage, until the day when Noah entered the ark, and the flood came and destroyed them all. Likewise as it was in the days of Lot—they ate, they drank, they bought, they sold, they planted, they built, but on the day when Lot went out from Sodom fire and brimstone rained from heaven and destroyed them all' " (Luke 17: 26-29, R.S.V.).

Besides all these things there would be *signs in the realm of religion.* For instance:

" 'This gospel of the kingdom shall be preached throughout the whole world, as a testimony to all nations; and then the end will come' " (Matthew 24:14, R.S.V.). In the same chapter He predicted that at His coming " 'all the tribes of the earth will mourn' "— indicative of the rejection of the gospel, and the final apostasy.

What about these promised signs? Do they have any meaning for us who live in the second half of the twentieth century?

As to the signs in the heavens—the darkening of the sun, the obscuring of the moon, and the falling of the stars—these all occurred decades ago, as explained in detail in my book *Your Bible and You.*

Happening when they did, they sent shock waves clear around the world, stimulating the religious revival of the early nineteenth century and setting the stage for the beginning of the great Second Advent Movement in 1844.

Concerning the *signs in the earth* it could be argued that there have always been wars, famines, pestilences, and earthquakes, so how could such calamities be regarded as indications of the approach of Christ's second coming? The answer is that when Christ made this prediction He was well aware of the continuing nature of human conflict and therefore must have had in mind the multiplication and expansion of these disasters as the world's population would grow with increasing rapidity toward the end.

With this in mind it becomes extremely significant that during the past half century the world has suffered from the greatest wars, famines, pestilences, and earthquakes since the dawn of time.

There have been wars in every century, but none so costly as World War I and World War II.

There have been famines all down the years, but none so deadly as those which have occurred in Russia, Pakistan, India, and China within living memory.

Pestilences may be under better control now than in the Middle Ages, but even so, untold millions die of disease every year in under-privileged countries.

As to earthquakes, there have been more major catastrophes of this sort since 1900 than in any previous century, mighty upheavals with appalling loss of life as if, to quote Paul's graphic phrase, "the whole created universe groans in all its parts" (Romans 8:22, N.E.B.).

As to "distress of nations, with perplexity," this is many times greater today than at any other period of history, partly because there are more nations to complicate matters, partly because of the population explosion, and partly because of the invention of atomic weapons, which in very truth cause men to faint with fear and foreboding at what is coming upon the earth.

And if the words "sea" and "waves" may be taken as symbolic of "peoples, and multitudes," as suggested in Revelation 17:15, then we have in this passage a truly astonishing forecast of the endless riots and revolutions, marches and counter-marches, so characteristic of the times in which we live. Amazingly accurate is the prediction that the nations will stand "helpless," not knowing which way to turn from the roar and surge of the sea.

Concerning the *signs in social affairs,* who would question their appearance in the many evidences of moral depravity so painfully obvious today? The sickening emphasis on sex in books, periodicals, newspapers, and movies, the appalling increase of divorce, the rising tide of crime, the growth of youthful vandalism and juvenile delinquency—all reveal a moral collapse unequaled since the fall of Rome, the end of the Babylonian Empire, the destruction of Sodom and Gomorrah, or the coming of the Flood upon the antediluvians.

The Bible says that in the days before the Flood "the earth . . . was corrupt" and "filled with violence" (Genesis 6:12, 13). Moreover, the decay had spread so far that "every imagination of the thoughts" of men's hearts was "only evil continually" (verse 5). How perfectly the words describe the moral tragedy of our day! Surely the wheel has turned full circle. The days of Noah are here again.

Coming now to *religious signs,* only today can it be said that the gospel has been preached throughout the whole world, as a testimony to all nations. This wasn't true in the fifth century or the tenth or the fifteenth. The world hadn't been explored in those days; Christians had not as yet caught the vision of taking the gospel to the ends of the earth; nor had they the means of getting there had they wished to go.

Proclaiming the gospel universally is a comparatively modern concept. So is universal Bible distribution. Not till the nineteenth century did missionaries go overseas in large numbers. Only recently did the American Bible Society celebrate its 150th anniversary, having succeeded in translating some part of the Holy Scriptures into more than 1,200 languages.

Now, too, as noted in a previous chapter, there has come upon the scene the great Second Advent Movement, with its sudden and dramatic outreach to "every nation, and kindred, and tongue, and people," exactly as predicted in Revelation 14:6, 7. Boldly it bears the very message God said would be given to the world just before the end: "Fear God, and give glory to him; for the hour of his judgment is come." Zealously it is gathering a people out of "Babylon"—"God's people"—who "keep the commandments of God, and the faith of Jesus" (verse 12).

Important, however, as are all these evidences of approaching climax, there is another sign that merits special attention at this time. I refer to the rapidly accelerating tempo of life, the way events of vast significance are occurring, one after another, at unprecedented speed.

Everybody is cognizant of it. "It's all so sudden" has become a common expression, so very typical of our times. All sorts of events that once seemed impossible, beyond all reason, are happening with breathtaking suddenness.

This too has a Biblical background, unique and fascinating.

Notice for a moment the two great oaths in the Bible, one in Genesis, the other in Revelation, but both linked intimately with the divine plan of salvation for mankind.

In Genesis the Lord said to Abraham, "By myself have I sworn . . . that in blessing I will bless thee, and in multiplying I will multiply thy seed as the stars of the heaven, and as the sand which is upon the sea shore; . . . and in thy seed shall all the nations of the earth be blessed" (chapter 22:16-18).

This most solemn promise gave assurance that the gospel of Christ would ultimately be carried to all the world as a blessing to all mankind.

In the book of Revelation appears the second great oath, where the Lord swears by Himself again—not now to Abraham but to all the world—that His plan of salvation will soon be consummated. He "raised his right hand to heaven and swore by him who lives for ever and ever, who created heaven and earth and the sea and everything in them: 'There shall be no more delay; but when the time comes for the seventh angel to sound his trumpet, the hidden purpose of God will have been fulfilled, as he promised to his servants the prophets'" (chapter 10:5-7, N.E.B.).

No more delay! In this dramatic declaration we catch a glimpse of the divine impatience for the end of sin, the intensity of Christ's yearning that the long controversy between good and evil be concluded.

There is to be no more delay in the fulfillment of prophecy, no more delay in giving God's last message to the world. His people are to bind off their work, to complete what remains to be completed and prepare for the final climactic scenes of the great drama of the ages.

When is this declaration made? Before the seventh angel sounds his trumpet, at which time "the kingdoms of this world" shall "become the kingdoms of our Lord, and of his Christ; and he shall reign for ever and ever" (Revelation 11:15).

It is therefore "in the days of these kings"—to use Daniel's phrase—that this divine edict goes forth. In our time. Now. Today the words echo and re-echo throughout the universe, from planet to planet, sun to sun, star to star, to the farthest limits of the realms of God: "There shall be no more delay!"

This is the reason for the sudden onrush of earth-shaking events that encompass and well-nigh overwhelm us in these tremendous times. Everywhere, in every aspect of life, the pace is quickening.

One senses it in the swiftness of modern travel, in man's ability to fly from place to place in almost no time at all. Pope Paul flew from Rome to New York, addressed the United Nations, met the President of the United States, said mass in Yankee Stadium, and flew back to Rome all in thirty-six hours.

When supersonic jets take to the air, traveling 2,000 miles an hour, passengers will arrive at their destination almost before they realize that they have left their home airport.

One also senses speed in the rapidity of modern communication, in man's ability to converse with his fellow man in all parts of the world by telephone, radio, television, and Telstar. When some celebrity appears on TV, hundreds of millions see and hear him simultaneously.

The general quickening is likewise apparent in the swift demise of great empires and the sudden emergence of dozens of new nations—the most amazing revolution in the history of the world and a definite fulfillment of the inspired prediction that all nations will "awake" in the judgment hour. See Joel 3:12-14.

236 GOOD NEWS FOR YOU

One cannot but notice a similar trend in the almost incredible changes that have taken place in the Roman Catholic Church during the past five years, changes that seemed utterly impossible even a decade ago. Inspired by Pope John XXIII, this ancient religious organization has taken a sudden leap into the twentieth century, as evidenced by many of the actions taken during Vatican II, including the epochal Declaration on Religious Liberty.

Equally affected by the hurricane of modern ideas are the non-Roman churches, which are being split asunder by the so-called unity movement, those willing for reunion at any price breaking away from those who hold that truth is more important than a fictitious "oneness."

The speed-up appears again in the swift progress of the great Second Advent Movement toward the fulfillment of its global objective. God said that it would go to all the world in the very last days with the speed of angels—like angels "flying in the midst of heaven"—and thus indeed it has gone, and is now going, to every nation.

Mysteriously, an awesome sense of urgency is gripping mankind. Speed and more speed is the order of the day. Events of vast importance occur with incredible rapidity. Even legislation that used to take years to get through Congress is swept through in days or weeks.

It is a sign of the times, perhaps the greatest sign of all. It tells us that time is running out, that there isn't much time left.

This means that there's not much time left to wait for the coming of the Lord. Sooner than we think, He will return in glory as King of kings and Lord of lords.

What good news is this!

For that will be a day of days, without precedent since time began.

For all who love the Lord it will be a day of hopes fulfilled and dreams come true.

The dead will be raised. Long-separated families will be reunited. Tears will give place to laughter, sadness to joy unbounded.

All pain will cease; so will all sorrow and heartache.

The sick will be healed in an instant, the maimed find missing limbs restored. "The eyes of the blind shall be opened, and the ears of the deaf shall be unstopped. Then shall the lame man leap as an hart, and the tongue of the dumb sing" (Isaiah 35:5, 6).

Cripples will bound from their wheel chairs. Polio victims will throw away their metal braces. Sufferers from arthritis and multiple sclerosis and Parkinson's disease will stand erect once more.

At the selfsame moment all that is evil, all that hurts

and harms, all that is unworthy of a place in God's kingdom of righteousness, will fade from sight and memory in the blazing radiance of His presence (2 Thessalonians 2:8).

What a day that will be! What a sublimely glorious, unforgettable day!

No wonder Jesus tells us to watch for it. It's something worth watching and waiting for, though the waiting now should not be long.

"Yes, I am coming soon!" He says.

With gladness let us respond, "Amen. Come, Lord Jesus!" (Revelation 22:20, N.E.B.).

Truly,

> "We know not the time when He cometh,
> At even, or midnight, or morn;
> It may be at deepening twilight;
> It may be at earliest dawn.
> He bids us to watch and be ready,
> Nor suffer our lights to grow dim,
> That when He shall come, He may find us
> All waiting and watching for Him."

19

Best News of All

NOT LONG ago I was standing on the balcony of my room in the Hotel Grand National in Lucerne, Switzerland, looking across the lake at the high Alps. It was a dull, cloudy day and the beauty of the peaks was veiled in mist. Now and then a snow-capped giant became visible, but only for a moment before clouds swept down and enveloped it once more.

Then all of a sudden, far off in the distance, a point of light appeared, brilliant and dazzling, its glory accentuated by the surrounding gloom. A lofty white pinnacle had caught the rays of the morning sun, becoming at once a signal of hope, a harbinger of brighter days to come.

Where I stood I could not see the sun, but the mountain saw it and flashed the good news everywhere that it was still shining.

That shaft of light revealed in glowing symbol the greatest news of all: that beyond this present life, so temporary, so shrouded in darkness, there is another, infinitely more glorious, which shall never end.

Eternal life is indeed what the gospel of Christ is all about. It is the center and soul of the good news He came to bring to the children of men.

" 'God loved the world so much,' " He told Nicodemus, " 'that he gave his only Son, that everyone who has faith in him may not die but have eternal life' " (John 3:16, N.E.B.).

This was the reason for Bethlehem, Calvary, and Olivet. The Holy Child was born that men might not die but live forever.

"I am come that they might have life," He said to His disciples, "and that they might have it more abundantly" (John 10:10).

" 'I have come that men may have life, and may have it in all its fullness' " is the rendering of the *New English Bible.*

Christ looked upon death as a great evil, as an enemy to be destroyed, so that it would no longer bring misery to mankind. As Author of life He alone could break the power of death. And this He did by rising from the dead in His own glorious resurrection. By this mighty act He let all men know that they could live again—if they would—and that He has the power to bring them back from the grave.

Life, inexplicable, mysterious, wonderful beyond words, was the greatest gift He gave to Adam. It is the most precious gift He gives to every human being today. And it will be the greatest gift He will bestow upon those who are raised from the dead, or translated, to become the citizens of His kingdom of righteousness. This new life will never have to be surrendered. It will never end, for in that glorious tomorrow death shall be no more. In that day it shall be said, "O death, where is thy sting? O grave, where is thy victory?" (1 Corinthians 15:55).

Here, then, is the best news of all: *You may live forever.*

One of the saddest things about this present life is that it is so very short—not nearly long enough to do all the things one wants to do. All too often a young man barely finishes his education before his life is snuffed out in a car accident or by an enemy bullet. Others attain a position they have worked for and dreamed about for decades only to learn they must exchange it for a hospital bed and a plot of earth in a cemetery. Sometimes a scientist is struck down on the very eve of a major discov-

16

ery, success seemingly only a week or two away. It is all so frustrating, so hard to understand and accept.

But in the future, when God's plans carry, it shall not be this way. There will be no interrupted programs or blasted hopes. Life will go on and on, for the Bible says, "As the days of a tree are the days of my people" (Isaiah 65:22). Not like a pine, which is comparatively short-lived, but like a redwood or a cedar of Lebanon, symbols of agelessness.

What of this life so generously offered, so fully guaranteed? Will it be worth living?

Of course it will, for it is unthinkable that millions of people should have to live forever in mounting dissatisfaction. Surely the One who planned so majestic a project, and paid so dearly to make it possible and workable, must have made provision that the endless years will be happy ones.

That there are many doubts about the nature of the life to come I freely admit, but for the most part they have been triggered by foolish and unfounded fantasies. All too often the "saved" have been pictured clad in long gowns, sitting on little pink clouds, playing harps through all eternity.

If this were heaven I would have to beg to be excused. I couldn't stand it—not for twenty-four hours, let alone a hundred million years! For one thing, I would hate to be in such an exposed position in such flimsy attire. For another, I would feel too insecure on that misty cloud, not knowing when it might evaporate in the sunshine. As for the harp, I would have to say No. I like the shape of a harp, but picking those strings for all eternity —I ask you! Playing a piano might be better, but who would want to do that through ages without end? And how would one hoist a piano onto a cloud anyway?

Such absurdities as these have spoiled God's beautiful plan in many people's minds. Such a heaven isn't worth the effort to get there.

Man's future home isn't going to be like this at all. Such fantasies are but cheap caricatures of the most lovely thing God ever conceived for the happiness of His creatures.

Calvary is an indication of how much He is prepared to do for the children of men, how far He is willing to go to help them in this life and the next. How foolish to suppose that He died to save them, to make everlasting life available to them, only to let them loose in a meaningless, purposeless vacuum for all eternity!

God *must* have had a glorious program in mind for man's future or He would not have embarked on the plan of redemption in the first place. Without such a program eternal life would be a worthless gift. And He *has* a program, marvelous beyond description, custom fitted to every person who desires to share in it.

Misunderstandings concerning it have arisen largely because of a misuse of the word "heaven." Sometimes, quite properly, we use the word when speaking of the sky above us, sometimes when speaking of God's dwelling place, as when Job said, "Is not God in the height of heaven?" (Job 22:12). But neither use has anything to do with the eternal home of the redeemed.

The home where people will enjoy eternal life will not be in some far-off region of space but right here on the earth. It will not be spooky and ethereal but real and substantial, as is the earth on which we stand today.

The Bible is most definite on this point.

"The heaven, even the heavens, are the Lord's," wrote the psalmist: "but *the earth* hath he given to the children of men" (Psalm 115:16).

"The earth he has assigned to men" is Dr. Moffatt's rendering.

Other statements read:

"Evildoers shall be cut off: but those that wait upon the Lord, they shall inherit *the earth*" (Psalm 37:9). "The righteous shall inherit *the land,* and dwell therein for ever" (verse 29).

Jesus declared, "Blessed are the meek: for they shall inherit *the earth*" (Matthew 5:5).

Nothing could be clearer. The earth will be man's future home, and it will be "heaven" only in the sense that it will be a place of unalloyed happiness.

Of course, it will not be the earth as we know it to-day, marred by man's sin and folly in so many ways. It will be the earth as remade by God, transformed so completely that it will outshine, if possible, the exquisite globe that came from the Creator's hand in the long ago.

This renewal was described by the apostle Peter in these dramatic words: "The day of the Lord will come as a thief in the night; in the which the heavens shall pass away with a great noise, and the elements shall melt with fervent heat, the earth also and the works that are therein shall be burned up. . . . Nevertheless we, according to his promise, look for new heavens and a new earth, wherein dwelleth righteousness" (2 Peter 3:10-13).

"On that day the heavens will disappear with a great rushing sound," says the *New English Bible;* "the elements will disintegrate in flames, and the earth with all that is in it will be laid bare. . . . But we have his promise, and look forward to new heavens and a new earth, the home of justice."

This would suggest some sort of atomic fission, a cleansing so thorough that even the atoms of the globe will be renewed, as indicated also in the prediction "Behold, I create new heavens and a new earth: and the former shall not be remembered, nor come into mind" (Isaiah 65:17).

The apostle John forecast the same total renovation when he said, "I saw a new heaven and a new earth: for the first heaven and the first earth were passed away" (Revelation 21:1).

There can be no question, therefore, that God's program includes the re-creation of this present earth into a gloriously beautiful home for His people, where they will enjoy all the blessings of eternal life.

This home has never been adequately described, even by the greatest of the Bible prophets. They did the best they could, but the task was beyond them. The apostle Paul realized this when he told the Corinthians, "Eye hath not seen, nor ear heard, neither have entered into the heart of man, the things which God hath prepared for them that love him" (1 Corinthians 2:9).

Dr. Moffatt renders this passage thus: "What no eye has ever seen, what no ear has ever heard, what never entered the mind of man, God has prepared all that for those who love him."

Either way, the thought is most intriguing. It suggests that God has prepared something superlatively wonderful, far beyond our present ability to comprehend, and we may rightly conclude that eternal life will be an utterly unprecedented experience, full of exciting surprises, thrilling discoveries, exquisite enjoyment, day after day, year after year, century after century, eon after eon, to all eternity.

It is because God's plans for man's future are so indescribably glorious that the prophets had so much difficulty in conveying even a few brief glimpses of what lies ahead. That's why they so often used symbolic language. Nothing else would suffice.

Fortunately, some of their predictions are easy to comprehend and appreciate. For instance, the prophet Isaiah says, "The inhabitant shall not say, I am sick" (Isaiah 33:24).

That's brief enough, but how much it comprehends! Nobody sick, ever! No more measles, mumps, chickenpox, tuberculosis, rheumatism, heart disease, or cancer. Not one of the diseases mentioned in the biggest medical dictionary will ever be seen again. There won't be a single hospital or dispensary anywhere, for there will be no patients. Medicare will be an obsolete concept, for eternal life will mean eternal health—vibrant, radiant, exuberant. Nobody will ever grow old. After a million years all will be young in heart, soul, and body.

The apostle John tells us that "God shall wipe away all tears from their eyes; and there shall be no more death, neither sorrow, nor crying, neither shall there be any more pain: for the former things are passed away" (Revelation 21:4).

This too we can understand. It will be a deathless world, with no funerals, no mortuaries, no caskets, no graves, no tears. In a thousand million years the sound of crying will never be heard again. Not anywhere for any reason. Nor will there be any more pain. No more headaches, backaches, toothaches—any kind of aches. No more agony from broken bones or broken hearts.

John also tells us that in that happy land there will be "the tree of life, which bare twelve manner of fruits, and yielded her fruit every month: and the leaves of the tree were for the healing of the nations" (Revelation 22:2). There is much symbolism here, but the deep truth behind it is apparent. There will be food enough for all. Nobody will ever have to go hungry. Consequently there will never be need of an anti-poverty program. Nobody will be poor. Abundant provision will be made for every possible contingency in the greatest social security system ever devised. Hence there will be no need for worry.

Peace of mind will be the perennial possession of all.

The prophet Ezekiel tells us that the people of that land will "dwell safely, all of them dwelling without walls, and having neither bars nor gates" (Ezekiel 38: 11). There is an ancient flavor to this prediction, with its reference to walls and gates, but here again the essential message is clear. In God's new world of tomorrow everybody will dwell safely. There will be no need for walls or gates, or even locks on doors. Nowhere in all that happy land will there be a single burglar or gangster or criminal of any kind. Crime will be nonexistent. Consequently there will be no law enforcement agencies, no law courts, no prisons. Why? Because no one will be there who has not consented to the vital clauses of God's new covenant, as described in Hebrews 8:10: "This is the covenant that I will make with the house of Israel after those days, saith the Lord; I will put my laws into their mind, and write them in their hearts: and I will be to them a God, and they shall be to me a people."

Only law-abiding people—with the love of God in their hearts—will live forever. It couldn't be otherwise. That's why the eternal world will be so peaceful, so free of strife and conflict—a place where men will "learn war" no more (Isaiah 2:4).

Along this same line the prophet Zephaniah says:

"The remnant of Israel shall not do iniquity, nor speak lies; neither shall a deceitful tongue be found in their mouth: for they shall feed and lie down, and none shall make them afraid" (Zephaniah 3:13). The home of the saved will be a land without fear. Nobody will ever have reason to be afraid day or night. There will be no need to fear invading armies, for there will be no armies. There will be no need to fear bandits, for there will be no bandits. And there will be no need to fear malicious gossip, because nobody will be there who speaks lies or has a "deceitful tongue."

When the prophets begin to describe living conditions in the eternal world, and the kind of homes people will have, their use of symbols becomes more pronounced. For instance, the prophet Isaiah says: "They shall build houses, and inhabit them; and they shall plant vineyards, and eat the fruit of them. They shall not build and another inhabit; they shall not plant, and another eat. . . . And mine elect shall long enjoy the work of their hands. They shall not labour in vain" (Isaiah 65:21-23).

This could not possibly mean that the saved will build houses and plant vineyards over and over again through all eternity. Who would want to do that anyway? This is a symbol of creative activity of all kinds. Everybody's talents will be used to the utmost in one way or

With this earth restored to its Edenic beauty, as promised
in the Bible, sin, sorrow, pain, and death will give place
to the eternal joy of the redeemed.

another. And their labor, whatever it may be, will not be in vain. It won't be taken over by somebody else. A person will be able to enjoy the work of his hands for a long, long time, even through all eternity.

The apostle John tells us that the New Jerusalem, capital of the beautiful new earth, will be a most glorious city. Indeed, when he saw it in vision he was so overcome that he began talking about foundations of precious stones, streets of gold, and gates of pearl—all symbols of sublime beauty, glory, radiance, and sheer breathtaking loveliness. It was so exquisite, he said, that it was like "a bride adorned for her husband." Everybody can understand that. Brides are invariably beautiful on their wedding day.

He assures us that there will be a tree-lined river running through the city, "a pure river of water of life, clear as crystal." I like that. It reminds me of lovely old Christchurch, New Zealand, where the river Avon, also tree-lined and beautifully landscaped, runs clear round the whole town. It also suggests the possibility of boating, for after all, if the inhabitants are going to "build houses" why shouldn't they also build boats?

Anyway, it's obvious that the New Jerusalem is going to be the most exquisite metropolis ever, far in advance of anything the modern city-renewal planners ever envisaged.

The home of the saints will be "no mean city" indeed.

All this, of course, is good news, wonderful news. In fact, what better news could you have than that God has planned such a delightful home where you may live forever in perfect happiness and peace? Surely He could have thought of nothing more to keep you joyously, totally satisfied through all eternity.

Yet there *is* something else. There is still other news for you which is even better than the best.

Says the apostle John: "The throne of God and of the Lamb shall be in it; and his servants shall serve him: and they shall see his face" (Revelation 22:3, 4).

Jesus Himself will be there. The Creator, Redeemer, and Lover of mankind will live with His people forever.

Long, long ago a poor blind man sat by the Jericho road, longing to see the earth, the trees, and the faces of his fellow men he had never looked upon. By and by he heard sounds as of a multitude coming toward him. There was much shouting and scraping of feet. All of a sudden there came to his ears the most wonderful news he had ever heard, "Jesus of Nazareth passes by!" His one great chance had come! At the top of his voice he cried, "Jesus, thou Son of David, have mercy upon me!"

Jesus heard him above the din of the crowd. He paused and spoke those power-filled words, "Receive thy sight!" The man's eyes opened. And there was Jesus! Face to face they stood there, looking at each other, One with boundless sympathy, the other with utter ecstasy. The Redeemer and the redeemed; the Lover and he who needed love so much.

So it will be through all eternity. Again and again we shall see Him face to face, ever with adoration and gratitude in our hearts.

This is what the poet had in mind when he wrote:

> "O heaven without my Saviour
> Would be no heaven to me;
> Dim were the walls of jasper
> Rayless the crystal sea."

Seeing Him there every day, knowing He is always near, will be the crowning fulfillment of the angel's promise of "great joy" to all people. There could be no greater joy than this.

No wonder we read, "The Spirit and the bride say, Come" (Revelation 22:17). The Lord wants us to accept all this good news as though He had offered it to us personally. He wants us to act upon it and make sure that all the wonderful things He has prepared for us will be ours.

Perhaps at this moment, by His Spirit, He is speaking

to you. He wants you to come. To give your heart to Him. To become one of His people. To link your life, your plans, your hopes, with His.

He has called you before. He is calling again now. Don't disappoint Him.

Not long ago I was at the London airport waiting for a plane to New York. As I stood there I became aware of a voice coming over the public-address system announcing a flight to Karachi, Bombay, Calcutta, Rangoon, and Singapore. The names fascinated me. Then the voice said, "This flight is awaiting the embarkation of the following nine passengers."

The names were read out and I thought that would be all. But it wasn't. Presently the voice spoke again. Once more the flight was announced, followed by these words: "There are still six passengers missing from this flight. Will they please proceed to the boarding gate immediately."

Fully five minutes later I heard the voice again. To my surprise the Singapore plane hadn't left yet. There were still three passengers missing. Naming the people once more, the voice said, "Will these three passengers please make their way to the boarding gate *now*."

I was sure this would be the last call, but it wasn't.

A few minutes later I heard the voice again, speaking

now with much greater urgency. "The flight to Karachi, Bombay, Calcutta, Rangoon, and Singapore is about to leave. There is one passenger still missing. Will he please come immediately. This is the final call."

I marveled at the patience of the airline officials. Then I thought of the patience of God, who has done such great things for us, who has planned such a wonderful journey and sent us such great good news about it all.

He is waiting now—for you! He is concerned as if you were the last missing passenger.

This could be His final call.

God sent not his Son into th

but that the world through